OPPOSING
VIEWPOINTS®
SERIES

# Women's Health

# Other Books of Related Interest

## Opposing Viewpoints Series

Abortion

Dietary Supplements

Gender Roles

Religious Liberty

## At Issue Series

The Affordable Care Act

Self-Defense Laws

Sexual Assault and the Military

Vaccines

## Current Controversies Series

Abortion

Drug Legalization

Medical Ethics

Same-Sex Marriage

"Congress shall make no law . . . abridging the freedom of speech, or of the press."

*First Amendment to the US Constitution*

The basic foundation of our democracy is the First Amendment guarantee of freedom of expression. The Opposing Viewpoints Series is dedicated to the concept of this basic freedom and the idea that it is more important to practice it than to enshrine it.

# OPPOSING VIEWPOINTS® SERIES

# Women's Health

*Lynn M. Zott, Book Editor*

**GREENHAVEN PRESS**
*A part of Gale, Cengage Learning*

GALE
CENGAGE Learning·

Farmington Hills, Mich • San Francisco • New York • Waterville, Maine
Meriden, Conn • Mason, Ohio • Chicago

Elizabeth Des Chenes, *Director, Content Strategy*
Douglas Dentino, *Manager, New Product*

*For more information, contact:*
Greenhaven Press
27500 Drake Rd.
Farmington Hills, MI 48331-3535
Or you can visit our Internet site at gale.cengage.com

**LIBRARY OF CONGRESS CATALOGING-IN-PUBLICATION DATA**

Women's health / Lynn M. Zott, book editor.
        pages cm. -- (Opposing viewpoints)
        Summary: "Opposing Viewpoints is the leading source for libraries and classrooms in need of current-issue materials. The viewpoints are selected from a wide range of highly respected sources and publications. This title in the series discusses the latest issues concerning the health of women."-- Provided by publisher.
        Includes bibliographical references and index.
        ISBN 978-0-7377-6668-4 (hardback) -- ISBN 978-0-7377-6669-1 (paperback)
        1. Women--Health and hygiene. I. Zott, Lynn M. (Lynn Marie), 1969-
    RA778.W6825 2015
    613'.04244--dc23
                                                                2014010758

Printed in the United States of America
1 2 3 4 5 6 7 18 17 16 15 14

# Contents

## Chapter 3: What Clinical Concerns Impact Women's Health?

**Chapter 4: What Are Key Health Issues That Affect US Servicewomen?**

# Why Consider Opposing Viewpoints?

> "The only way in which a human being can make some approach to knowing the whole of a subject is by hearing what can be said about it by persons of every variety of opinion and studying all modes in which it can be looked at by every character of mind. No wise man ever acquired his wisdom in any mode but this."
>
> *John Stuart Mill*

In our media-intensive culture it is not difficult to find differing opinions. Thousands of newspapers and magazines and dozens of radio and television talk shows resound with differing points of view. The difficulty lies in deciding which opinion to agree with and which "experts" seem the most credible. The more inundated we become with differing opinions and claims, the more essential it is to hone critical reading and thinking skills to evaluate these ideas. Opposing Viewpoints books address this problem directly by presenting stimulating debates that can be used to enhance and teach these skills. The varied opinions contained in each book examine many different aspects of a single issue. While examining these conveniently edited opposing views, readers can develop critical thinking skills such as the ability to compare and contrast authors' credibility, facts, argumentation styles, use of persuasive techniques, and other stylistic tools. In short, the Opposing Viewpoints Series is an ideal way to attain the higher-level thinking and reading skills so essential in a culture of diverse and contradictory opinions.

In addition to providing a tool for critical thinking, Opposing Viewpoints books challenge readers to question their own strongly held opinions and assumptions. Most people form their opinions on the basis of upbringing, peer pressure, and personal, cultural, or professional bias. By reading carefully balanced opposing views, readers must directly confront new ideas as well as the opinions of those with whom they disagree. This is not to argue simplistically that everyone who reads opposing views will—or should—change his or her opinion. Instead, the series enhances readers' understanding of their own views by encouraging confrontation with opposing ideas. Careful examination of others' views can lead to the readers' understanding of the logical inconsistencies in their own opinions, perspective on why they hold an opinion, and the consideration of the possibility that their opinion requires further evaluation.

## Evaluating Other Opinions

To ensure that this type of examination occurs, Opposing Viewpoints books present all types of opinions. Prominent spokespeople on different sides of each issue as well as well-known professionals from many disciplines challenge the reader. An additional goal of the series is to provide a forum for other, less known, or even unpopular viewpoints. The opinion of an ordinary person who has had to make the decision to cut off life support from a terminally ill relative, for example, may be just as valuable and provide just as much insight as a medical ethicist's professional opinion. The editors have two additional purposes in including these less known views. One, the editors encourage readers to respect others' opinions—even when not enhanced by professional credibility. It is only by reading or listening to and objectively evaluating others' ideas that one can determine whether they are worthy of consideration. Two, the inclusion of such viewpoints encourages the important critical thinking skill of objectively evaluating an author's credentials and bias. This evaluation will illuminate an author's reasons for taking a particular stance on an issue and will aid in readers' evaluation of the author's ideas.

It is our hope that these books will give readers a deeper understanding of the issues debated and an appreciation of the complexity of even seemingly simple issues when good and honest people disagree. This awareness is particularly important in a democratic society such as ours in which people enter into public debate to determine the common good. Those with whom one disagrees should not be regarded as enemies but rather as people whose views deserve careful examination and may shed light on one's own.

Thomas Jefferson once said that "difference of opinion leads to inquiry, and inquiry to truth." Jefferson, a broadly educated man, argued that "if a nation expects to be ignorant and free . . . it expects what never was and never will be." As individuals and as a nation, it is imperative that we consider the opinions of others and examine them with skill and discernment. The Opposing Viewpoints Series is intended to help readers achieve this goal.

*David L. Bender and Bruno Leone,*
*Founders*

# Introduction

*"Women are more likely than men to suffer from multiple chronic conditions, and women are in greater need of health care services across their lifespan."*

—US Department of
Health and Human Services,
Office on Women's Health

In June 2013 a battle ensued in the Texas Senate chambers between Republican state senators and Wendy Davis, a Democratic state senator, over a bill banning abortions after the twentieth week of a pregnancy. The bill required women who take pills to induce abortion to ingest them in a doctor's presence at a certified abortion facility (as stated in federal regulations for the pills), and required all clinics performing abortions to be licensed as ambulatory surgical centers. Davis famously filibustered for thirteen hours straight, standing and speaking out against the bill while sporting athletic shoes to aid her in adhering to the rules that prevented her from either leaning or taking breaks to use the restroom. The bill, Davis argued, would severely limit access to abortions in the state, as the minimum standards for licensure as an ambulatory surgical center, which include requiring doctors who perform abortions to have admitting privileges at a hospital no more than thirty miles from the clinic, are largely out of reach for many of the state's clinics, which lack the financial resources to upgrade, and their doctors, who are unlikely to be granted admitting privileges because they do not bring in business for hospitals due to the lack of complications from abortions. Supporters of the bill, which passed easily in the Texas House of Representatives, argue that the regulations save women's lives and safeguard their health by ensuring that they have access to on-site emergency care if they need it, but opponents of the bill echo the sentiments of Davis, who asked at one point during her filibuster, "What purpose does this bill serve? And could it be, might it just be a desire to limit women's access to safe, healthy, legal, constitutionally protected abortions in the state of Texas?"[1]

Although Davis's filibuster was successful in delaying the vote, the bill passed when Governor Rick Perry called a special legislative session to vote on it and then signed it into law, taking effect in October 2013. Portions of the law were challenged in federal district court and were ruled unconstitutional by district judge Lee Yeakel, who stated, "The admitting-privileges provision of House Bill 2 does not bear a rational relationship to the legitimate right of the state in preserving and promoting fetal life or a woman's health and, in any event, places a substantial obstacle in the path of a woman seeking an abortion of a nonviable fetus and is thus an undue burden to her." Yeakel added, "The medication abortion provision may not be enforced against any physician who determines, in appropriate medical judgment, to perform the medication-abortion using off-label protocol for the preservation of the life or health of the mother."[2] Governor Perry released a statement after the verdict, declaring, "Today's decision will not stop our ongoing efforts to protect life and ensure the women of our state aren't exposed to any more of the abortion-mill horror stories that have made headlines recently. We will continue fighting to implement the laws passed by the duly-elected officials of our state, laws that reflect the will and values of Texans."[3]

Despite Judge Yeakel's ruling, the law went into effect in October 2013, and on November 1, 2013, a three-judge panel in the US Fifth Circuit Court of Appeals refused to uphold the lower court judge's injunction against full enforcement of the law. Pro-life advocates rejoiced, like Townhall.com contributor Cortney O'Brien, who exulted, "Thanks to this newly enforced legislation . . . a dozen abortion clinics in the state are set to close—nine of which have already shuttered. Get ready for a whole lot more encouraging numbers."[4] Pro-choice advocates lamented the same statistics that O'Brien celebrated, and mourned what they viewed as a crushing blow to women's health and constitutional rights. Planned Parenthood president Cecile Richards, daughter of former Texas governor Ann Richards, commented, "This restriction clearly violates Texas women's constitutional rights by drastically reducing access to safe and legal abortion statewide."[5] Reports began to surface of women being turned away from clinics at which they had had appointments for abortions, as well as stories of women with serious health challenges being forced to cross state lines and travel long distances to obtain abortions that they needed to have for their own health reasons or because of their unborn child's devastating illnesses. Women's advocacy group UltraViolet put the closure of Texas clinics into perspective on November 14, 2013, tweeting a graphic titled "How the Texas Abortion Law Makes Choice Unaffordable" that declared "Women in poverty account for 40% of all abortions. HB2 hurts them most." The UltraViolet graphic also illustrates how a woman from El Paso, Texas, now has to travel 560 miles, 16 hours by car, to a San Antonio abortion provider. This trip, the picture states, would cost this woman $139.92 in gas, plus $500 for the abortion, for a total of $639.92, or 88.5 hours of work for minimum wage. The appeals court's decision to allow the law to go into effect is only temporary, and a federal appeals court in New Orleans began hearing arguments in January 2014 on whether Texas can enforce the law, but at this writing a third of Texas abortion clinics have been shut down.

Women's reproductive freedom is just one of the many issues related to women's health debated in *Opposing Viewpoints: Women's Health*. In chapters titled "What Is the Relationship Between Politics and Women's Health?," "What Should Be the Role of Religion in Women's Health Care

Policy?," "What Clinical Concerns Impact Women's Health?," and "What Are Key Health Issues That Affect US Servicewomen?," viewpoint authors cover such issues as the impact of laws and government on women's health, the intersection between faith and health policy, the medical community's ongoing debate over the appropriate methods of screening for illnesses and providing preventive services, and the issues confronting military women as their numbers increase and the armed forces manage their unique health concerns, on base, in combat arenas, and after discharge.

## Notes

1. Laura Bassett, "Wendy Davis, Texas Democrat, Fights Abortion Bill with 13-Hour Filibuster," *Huffington Post*, June 26, 2013. www.huffingtonpost.com/2013/06/25/wendy-davis-filibuster_n_3498699.html.

2. Chris Tomlinson, "Texas Abortion Restrictions Declared Unconstitutional by Federal Judge," *Huffington Post*, October 28, 2013. www.huffingtonpost.com/2013/10/28/texas-abortion-unconstitutional_n_4171087.html

3. Rick Perry, "Statement by Governor Perry on Abortion Law Ruling," October 28, 2013. http://rickperry.org/release/statement-gov-perry-abortion-law-ruling.

4. Cortney O'Brien, "Meanwhile in Texas: Abortion Appointments Canceled, Clinics Closing All Across State," Townhall.com, November 9, 2013. http://townhall.com/tipsheet/cortneyobrien/2013/11/09/meanwhile-in-texas-abortion-appointments-canceled-clinics-closing-all-across-state-n1743247.

5. Quoted in Cheryl K. Chumley, "12 Texas Abortion Clinics Closed as Appeals Court Upholds New Law," *Washington Times*, November 1, 2013. www.washingtontimes.com/news/2013/nov/1/texas-abortion-clinics-closed-appeals-court/.

OPPOSING
VIEWPOINTS®
SERIES

CHAPTER 1

# What Is the Relationship Between Politics and Women's Health?

# Chapter Preface

In November 2013 Senator Richard Blumenthal, joined by Senators Barbara Boxer and Tammy Baldwin and Representatives Marcia Fudge, Judy Chu, and Lois Frankel, introduced the Women's Health Protection Act of 2013 into Congress. The bill's supporters hope to provide a federal legal remedy for what are known as Targeted Regulation of Abortion Providers (TRAP) laws, such as some that have been passed in recent years requiring women seeking abortion services to first undergo, and in some cases watch, ultrasounds of their uterus; requiring facilities providing abortion services to be equipped and licensed as surgical centers; requiring a twenty-four-hour waiting period before having an abortion; and requiring doctors to discuss alternatives to abortion with patients before performing the procedure. Despite the 1973 US Supreme Court ruling in *Roe* v. *Wade* making it unconstitutional for states to prevent a woman from obtaining an abortion while the fetus is not yet viable (cannot live) outside the womb, many state laws are so restrictive, Blumenthal and his colleagues argue, that they effectively bar women's access to safe abortion services. Blumenthal argues,

> A new federal law is necessary to stop anti-choice legislators from using women's health and safety as a ploy to enact unconscionable and unconstitutional state statutes that obstruct and block women from essential health-care and reproductive rights. Such restrictions create cascading doubt and deception that deter women from making personal decisions based on their own values and constitutional rights. The Women's Health Protection Act invalidates unnecessary, unwarranted requirements and procedures—ranging from ultrasounds and admitting privileges to physical clinic layouts. . . . I am determined to stand with women against state laws abhorrent and antithetical to well-established rights. This law will help make reproductive rights real.

While the law, if passed, would not overturn state laws, it would offer a legal remedy for those who challenge the laws in court, as well as giving judges the capacity to examine such issues as the legality of restrictions in terms of whether they interfere with a doctor's ability to exercise medical judgment in good faith and in terms of whether they block women's access to legal abortion services. Boxer asserted, "The Women's Health Protection Act . . . affirms the fundamental principle that a woman's medical decisions are best left up to her, her family, and her doctor—not politicians waging radical assaults on women's reproductive health."

Political and legal battles over women's health are discussed at length in the following chapter, which covers the often polar-opposite positions of political parties on issues such as women's reproductive freedom and public funding for women's reproductive health services.

*"It's patronizing to think that using different language, new messaging, and female spokespersons will convince women to support a party that is so clearly working against their best interests."*

# The Republican Party's Policies Threaten Women's Health and Personal Freedom

### Andrea Flynn

*Andrea Flynn is a Roosevelt Institute fellow and a researcher and writer specializing in access to reproductive care. In the following viewpoint, she contends that Republicans' efforts to rebrand themselves as supporters of women's rights have no chance of succeeding because of anti-women's-rights policy decisions advanced by Republican lawmakers across the United States. She details various laws and initiatives that she maintains restrict women's access to health care and deprive them of reproductive freedom. In addition, Flynn argues, Republicans support massive budget cuts and the repeal of laws like the Affordable Care Act, which provide health care for women. Despite the party's efforts*

Andrea Flynn, "Why the GOP's Efforts to Reach Out to Women Are Doomed to Fail," *The Next New Deal: The Blog of the Roosevelt Institute*, March 20, 2013. Copyright © 2013 by The Roosevelt Institute. All rights reserved. Reproduced by permission.

*to cast itself in the role of defender of families and women's interests, Flynn says, their actions have alienated women, and women will not support a party that does not support them.*

As you read, consider the following questions:

1. What do Republicans plan to remind voters of during Women's History Month, according to Flynn?

2. How many clinics does the author say have been closed in Texas due to budget cuts and funding restrictions?

3. How many states, according to Flynn, restrict abortion coverage in health plans offered through insurance exchanges?

*W*hy should women vote for a party that's actively working against their needs and interests?

On Monday [March 18, 2013], the GOP [Republican Party] released a report detailing its "Growth and Opportunity Project," a new initiative that explores reasons for the party's November [2012] defeat and posits strategies for winning future elections. If it wasn't evident before, it is now abundantly clear that the Republican establishment officially attributes its November loss to a failure in style, not substance. The 100-page report details the party's inability to effectively communicate its policies and priorities to women, immigrants, young people, and people of color. It largely ignores the possibility that what motivated the majority of American voters, and in particular women, to give President [Barack] Obama a second term was an aversion to the GOP's outdated vision for the nation.

Acknowledging that Obama won the single women's vote by a "whopping 36 percent," the report's authors suggest ways the party can be more inclusive of this critical voting bloc: Making a better effort to listen to female voters; fighting against the Democratic rhetoric against the "so-called War on

Women"; doing a better job communicating the GOP's policies and employing female spokespeople to do it; and using Women's History Month to "remind voters of the Republican's Party historical role in advancing the women's rights movement."

## Advancing an Extreme Agenda

I'm glad they specified "historical" role in advancing the women's rights movement, given that their current role seems squarely focused on rolling back women's rights. It's encouraging that GOP strategists in Washington want to spend more time listening to women voters, but there is no indication that Republican lawmakers will respond to that feedback. As [MSNBC talk-show host] Rachel Maddow said on her program [*The Rachel Maddow Show*] this week, while Beltway [DC] leaders are "preaching about how to appear more reasonable to the women folk among us," Republican governance has become a competition—a race—"to see who can get the most extreme the fastest."

And a race it is.

This week Andrew Jenkins of [the alternative news site] RH Reality Check reported on some of the most recent Republican efforts to chip away at women's access to care:

> Arkansas just passed a bill banning abortions after 12 weeks of pregnancy, while South Dakota just passed a bill to expand its 72-hour waiting period, which was already one of the longest in the country, in a state with only one abortion clinic. The North Dakota Senate just approved a ban on abortions after six-weeks of pregnancy, the most restrictive in the country. And in Kansas, a state House committee just passed a 70-page bill that defines life at fertilization and requires that physicians lie to their patients.

That's not all.

## Republicans, Women, and Health Care

Republicans in Texas remain hard at work leading national efforts in steamrolling access to women's health care. Previous budget cuts and funding restrictions have already closed more than 50 clinics and are making it more difficult, if not impossible, for nearly 200,000 women to access care. Last week the Texas Senate Education Committee moved a bill forward that would ban Planned Parenthood and other organizations from providing sexuality education in schools, and the governor recently promised to advance a 20-week abortion ban.

In Wisconsin, four Planned Parenthood clinics closed as a result of a GOP-led ban that prevents the organization and other clinics from receiving state funds. In Oklahoma, a major Planned Parenthood facility closed after the state's department of health cut off funding through the WIC [Women, Infants, and Children] program, forcing low-income women to go elsewhere to obtain vouchers for themselves and their children. Last month [February 2013], Republicans in Michigan introduced a bill that would require women to get a vaginal ultrasound at least two hours before obtaining an abortion.

Mississippi is about to close its only abortion clinic thanks to a requirement that abortion doctors have admitting privileges at a local hospital (and local hospitals' refusal to grant those privileges)—a move the Republican governor has applauded as being the first step in ending abortion in that state. Earlier this year, a Republican (female!) representative in New Mexico proposed legislation that would have allowed for women who terminated pregnancies resulting from rape to be charged with a felony for tampering with evidence. (She promptly rescinded and then proposed a new bill that would instead charge abortion providers with facilitating the destruction of evidence.)

## The GOP Proposal to Care for Women

The new GOP report also suggested that Republicans "talk about people and families, not just numbers and statistics." In

## Republicans Aim to Restrict Women's Reproductive Freedom

Today, there's a national discourse raging around access to birth control—40 years after the Supreme Court legalized contraception for all women, irrespective of marital status, and five decades after the birth-control pill's introduction. And while fringy far-right extremists have always blasted away at contraceptive use, they have now infiltrated the mainstream—in the form of Tea Party Republicans and GOP presidential candidates. . . .

Some of the recent attacks launched by staunch conservatives are chillingly retro and misogynistic [women hating]: [2012 Republican presidential candidate] Rick Santorum's financial backer pining for the days when a woman stuck an aspirin between her knees to avoid pregnancy, . . . a panel of all-male House Republican legislators and religious leaders debating contraceptive coverage at a House Committee meeting; conservative radio host Rush Limbaugh going on a three-day on-air tirade against law student Sandra Fluke, calling her a slut and a prostitute for speaking up in favor of birth-control coverage. And . . . Republican presidential candidate Mitt Romney pledging to defund Planned Parenthood if elected.

*Gretchen Voss,* Women's Health, *September 2012.*

releasing his 2014 budget proposal last week, Paul Ryan certainly provided an interesting perspective into how the GOP proposes taking care of women and families. According to the National Women's Law Center (NWLC), the Ryan budget includes significant reductions for "child care and Head Start, K–12 education and Pell grants, job training, civil rights enforcement, women's preventive health care, domestic violence prevention and more." It would dismantle Medicaid, Medicare, and the food stamp program. It would repeal the Affordable Care Act (ACA), denying nearly 15 million women access to affordable health insurance and Medicaid and forcing women to pay more for prescription drugs, including family planning. As NWLC pointed out, repealing the ACA would "allow insurance companies to continue charging women higher premiums than men, deny coverage to women with so-called pre-existing conditions like domestic violence, and refuse to cover maternity care."

The ACA is certainly providing fertile ground for GOP lawmakers to show how much they care about women. Twenty states now restrict abortion coverage in health insurance plans that will be offered through the insurance exchanges, and 18 states restrict abortion coverage in insurance plans for public employees. Nearly all of those states are Republican-led. Additionally, 14 Republican governors have reported they will not participate in the Medicaid expansion programs that are a critical part of the ACA, denying access to a broad range of health services to millions of women.

On top of all this, 22 Republican Senators and 138 Republican members of the House voted last month against the Violence Against Women Act, a critical piece of legislation that provides assistance to victims of domestic and sexual violence.

## The GOP Will Not Fool Women Voters

In their report, the GOP strategists recommended developing training programs in messaging, communications, and recruiting that address the best ways to communicate with women. "Our candidates, spokespeople and staff need to use language that addresses concerns that are on women's minds in order to let them know we are fighting for them," they state. Given the abovementioned pieces of legislation, the GOP will be hard-pressed to convince women the party is fighting for them. It's patronizing to think that using different language, new messaging, and female spokespersons will convince women to support a party that is so clearly working against their best interests. Women are smart enough to know that a party that calls itself home to lawmakers relentlessly fighting to chip away at family planning and abortion access, food stamps, affordable health care, education, civil rights, and a social safety net providing tenuous stability to millions of marginalized individuals is not a party committed to truly understanding or addressing their priorities.

Maybe next year the GOP will attempt a more earnest effort at celebrating Women's History Month. Although, by that time, their state leaders might have alienated half the women in the country, and it will be too late.

*"By the Democrats' logic, to oppose abortion on demand and taxpayer-funded contraception is to be 'anti-woman.' Womanhood is thus defined by the desire for unrestricted abortion and free birth control; women themselves are reducible to ovaries."*

# The Democratic Party's Policies Threaten Women's Health and Personal Freedom

## Meghan Clyne

*Meghan Clyne is a writer and the managing editor of* National Affairs. *In the following viewpoint, she argues that Democrats' political platforms and policies reduce women's interests to reproductive health and freedom and do women a disservice by ignoring the issues that truly affect their well-being. Obamacare, she says, will negatively impact women's access to health care, and make it more difficult for them to run small businesses. Democrats' expansion of social programs like Medicaid and food stamps, Clyne contends, create a culture of perpetual dependency among women, preventing them from taking control of their own lives. By opposing faith-based groups' desire to preserve their religious freedom, she asserts, Democrats prevent these groups from providing much-needed assistance to women and goes against the beliefs of the majority of American women who oppose abortion. The Republican platform, Clyne concludes, would empower women and address their real needs for employment and financial stability, so that they can make decisions about their own well-being.*

As you read, consider the following questions:

1. According to Clyne, what issue did men and women list as the most important problem facing the country in a 2012 Gallup poll?

2. What percentage of women reported attending church "frequently" in a 2010 Gallup poll, as reported by the author?

3. What was the percentage of single-parent households headed by women living in poverty, according to 2010 Census Bureau data, as reported by Clyne?

In the sixth century B.C., the Chinese tactician Sun Tzu observed: "All warfare is based on deception." If only he could have seen the "war on women." This whopping deception— that Republicans are out to destroy women and everything they hold dear—looks increasingly like the Democrats' entire battle plan heading into [the elections in] November [2012]. For well over a year, party leaders, strategists, and elected officials have tried to rekindle hostilities at every opportunity— congressional votes on abortion, debates over the Obama-care contraceptive mandate, the selection of Paul Ryan as the Republican vice presidential nominee, and, most recently, Missouri congressman Todd Akin's bizarre comments on rape. Leaving nothing to doubt, the Democrats have orchestrated their convention agenda to press the same case: Speakers include Nancy Keenan, president of NARAL Pro-Choice

America; Cecile Richards, president of Planned Parenthood; and Sandra Fluke, who, as a 30-year-old Georgetown law student, became a household name by demanding free birth-control pills.

This is more than just stroking an important constituency: Democrats are making the "war on women" the centerpiece of their case for reelection. The motivations are as much tactical as ideological; young, unmarried women did not turn out for Democrats in the 2010 cycle, and if they stay home in 2012, it could spell doom for Obama's hopes of a second term.

## Democrats Focus on Reproduction

In the meantime, a perceptive observer may notice a curious thing about this "war on women." It is based entirely on one set of policies: those pertaining to women's reproductive systems. By the Democrats' logic, to oppose abortion on demand and taxpayer-funded contraception is to be "anti-woman." Womanhood is thus defined by the desire for unrestricted abortion and free birth control; women themselves are reducible to ovaries.

It was once permissible in American politics to view women as incapable of concerns beyond childbearing—but not in this century. And in addition to insulting women's intelligence, this approach may well backfire. American women are active, thoughtful citizens; their political concerns are focused on the future of their nation, not the cheapest and easiest way to shut down their reproductive tracts.

There is thus good reason to believe that the party that takes women seriously—speaking to them about their true aspirations for themselves, their families, and their country—will do better in November. So it is worth dispensing with gender-war deceptions to ask a much more relevant question: What do women really want—and which governing vision will best help them achieve it?

## The War on Opportunity

It's ironic that so-called feminists have caricatured women's voting priorities as the "girl issues." In truth, women's prime concerns in this election cycle are the same as men's, and can be summed up in two words: the economy.

In an August [2012] Gallup poll, voters were asked to identify the most important problem facing the country today. Men and women listed the same top two issues: the economy in general (32 percent men, 30 percent women), and unemployment/jobs (22 percent men, 25 percent women). ("Abortion issues" fell near the very bottom, failing to register even one half of one percent.)

[President Barack] Obama's record on the economy and jobs is nothing short of dismal. After nearly four years and trillions of dollars of spending and "stimulus," the unemployment rate in July [2012] was exactly the same as the rate in Obama's first full month in office: 8.3 percent. Flatlining job prospects are discouraging for everyone, but the numbers are particularly discouraging for women. In an economy in which underemployment is a staggering 17 percent, many women have had to settle for part-time work. The unemployment rate for people age 20 and older seeking full-time work is higher among women than men—8.4 percent versus 8.0 percent. For young, unmarried women supporting themselves—the demographic Obama is targeting with the "war on women"—unlimited free birth control is poor consolation for not having a full-time job. . . .

## Obama-Care Will Burden Women

One service that women consume much more than men do is health care—"poor health care" ranks high on their list of the nation's problems—and the Obama record here barely needs explanation. Obama-care will force millions of families out of the insurance plans they have now, reduce the quality of care, and introduce delays, rationing, and inefficiencies throughout the system. In selling the law, Democrats often noted that women make most health care decisions in America; moreover, mothers are more likely to wait with sick children at pediatricians' offices, and daughters are more likely to care for aging parents. As seeking medical care becomes more difficult and time-consuming—all for worse health outcomes and lower patient satisfaction—the pain will be more intense for American women.

Obama-care's employer mandates also make life much more difficult for women who are starting and running their own businesses. Indeed, the Obama agenda in general is a disaster for entrepreneurs, men and women alike. The president has promised to raise taxes on "the rich"—anyone making more than $200,000 a year. But according to a study from earlier this year by the National Federation of Independent Business, about 75 percent of the nation's small businesses are structured as "pass-through" businesses that report income and losses on owners' personal income-tax returns. This means that business income is assessed at the owners' personal rates. As a result of Obama's pledge and taxes that will go into effect as part of Obama-care, the top marginal tax rate will climb from 35 percent to 44 percent at the beginning of next year. For small-business owners, it's that much less money to invest in capital purchases and new hires. And as a 2010 Department of Commerce report (prepared for Obama's own White House Council on Women and Girls) noted, businesses owned by women tend to be smaller and start smaller than male-owned businesses. Obama's tax policies will thus disproportionately harm women entrepreneurs. . . .

## The War on Self-Determination

Women want jobs and economic opportunity, just as men do. Still, there are some policy issues that disproportionately affect women or are of special concern to them; in evaluating the Democrats' agenda, these merit consideration, too.

Consider, for instance, the administration's vast expansion of federal welfare programs. Enrollment for Medicaid, Temporary Assistance for Needy Families (TANF), the Supplemental Nutrition Assistance Program (SNAP), and the Women, Infants, and Children program have all increased dramatically under President Obama. Part of the increase understandably results from the dismal economy, but much of it can be attributed to stretched eligibility requirements and increased per-person benefits. These expansions have raised the effective marginal cost of finding a low-paying job (and thereby losing welfare benefits), giving beneficiaries greater incentive to remain on the dole. Indeed, in the case of food stamps, the administration has actively recruited participants—going so far as to use the White House faith-based office to pressure churches into using religious services and facilities to sign people up for SNAP.

A huge increase in welfare is a problem for the nation, but it's particularly damaging to women. These programs are designed to cover mostly women and their dependent children; as the programs have grown, so has the number of women reliant on them. When the 1996 welfare reform converted Aid to Families with Dependent Children to TANF—introducing work requirements and limiting welfare benefits to five years—it meant that millions of women, including many mothers, went back to work and took greater control over their own lives. This is real progress for women—progress that Obama's welfare-expanding policies would reverse.

And with long-lasting effects. Decades of experience have shown that welfare begets cycles of dependency that stretch across generations; daughters and granddaughters collect benefits from the same welfare offices as their mothers and grandmothers. No little girl in America should say, "I want to be a ward of the state when I grow up." Increasingly, however, it seems this is what President Obama envisions for them.

The starkest example came in the now-infamous "Life of Julia" slideshow published by the Obama campaign, meant to show how the president's policies would help a supposedly typical American female. What it illustrated was a woman dependent on the government from cradle to grave—for education, work, investment capital, health care, retirement income, and, of course, birth control. This is hardly an inspiring vision of women's empowerment.

## Democrats' Antireligious Bias

As if to prove the point, Obama administration policies have undermined organizations that help lift women out of poverty without forcing them to become dependent on the state. The administration's assault on religious freedom has imperiled faith-based charities that serve women with a humanity and compassion that no government bureaucracy can match. For example, the archbishop of Chicago, Francis Cardinal George, has warned that the HHS [US Dept. of Health and Human Services] contraceptive mandate might well force the city's Catholic social services to close down. In Barack Obama's own backyard, women may no longer have access to archdiocesan programs that support pregnant women and teens and provide counseling and case management for victims of domestic violence. Across the country, countless women being educated, healed, and supported by religious schools, hospitals, and charities may see these lifelines cut by Obama's policies.

The "war on women" narrative smears the Catholic church for being rigid about "women's issues." But it's the Obama administration insisting that, if religious institutions don't conform to the administration's orthodoxy on abortion and contraception, they can't continue providing other services that meet women's very real needs. Obama's assault on religious freedom may also make for bad politics: Historically, research has shown women to be more religious and involved in congregational life than men; a 2010 Gallup poll showed that 47 percent of women reported attending church "frequently"—"at least once a week" or "almost every week"—compared to 39 percent of men. Undermining the work of churches, and forcing them into protracted legal battles, harms institutions that matter disproportionately to women.

This points to the common fallacy that on "culture war" issues—marriage, family, and sex—Democrats are on the side of women, while Republicans seek (to borrow a [vice president Joe] Bidenism) to put them back in chains. Painful experience shows this to be untrue. Family breakdown—climbing divorce rates, the rise of unwed parenting—disproportionately harms women, who head nearly 80 percent of single-parent families. Aside from the emotional strain of single parenting, and the demonstrably poorer outcomes for children, the economic harm is significant. Census data from 2010 found the percentage of married parents living below the poverty line to be just 8.8 percent; for single-parent households headed by men, the number was 24.2 percent. But for single-parent households headed by women, an astonishing 40.7 percent were living in poverty.

Those peddling the "war on women" might argue that this is precisely why women need more access to abortion and contraceptives—so that they can avoid being unmarried parents. But access to contraception and abortion has been treated by the law as a constitutional right since *Griswold* v. *Connecticut* in 1965 and *Roe* v. *Wade* in 1973. And strangely enough, it was right around that time that the out-of-wedlock birthrate began to climb dramatically. In 1970, the percentage of births to unmarried mothers was around 10 percent, compared with more than 40 percent today; making it easier for unmarried women to avoid babies seems to have had exactly the opposite effect. If the goal is to help women avoid the impoverishment of single motherhood, the Democrats' preferred approach—more contraception and abortion—hasn't worked so far. The Republicans' approach—traditional, married child-rearing—offers more promise.

Besides, for all the allegations that Republican opposition to abortion constitutes a "war on women," most women themselves don't even support the practice. A Gallup poll in May showed that slightly more women describe themselves as "pro-life" than "pro-choice"—46 percent to 44 percent. Overall, America is a pro-life nation; on the questions of late-term and taxpayer-funded abortions, other polls show public opposition becoming even more intense.

On this issue, President Obama is well out of the mainstream. A clarifying episode came this May, when legislation to ban sex-selective abortion failed to secure the necessary two-thirds support in the House of Representatives because of Democratic opposition. Obama's White House piled on, releasing a statement saying the president, too, opposed the ban.

Martial metaphors are vastly overused, and the "war on women" is no exception. But if any policy amounts to a "war on women," surely allowing sex-selective abortion, which overwhelmingly targets unborn girls for the sole offense of possessing XX chromosomes, must be it.

## Republican Policies Favor Women

Historically, Democrats have had a strong electoral advantage among women, and the polls going into November [2012] suggest similar trends. But for [Republican presidential candidate] Mitt Romney, the challenge is not insurmountable: He and his running mate [Representative Paul Ryan] just need to convince enough female voters that the "war on women" is bogus, that President Obama has little to offer them, and that Republicans will do more to deliver on what American women really want.

There are signs that Romney and Ryan understand the task before them. During an interview at the Republican Convention, NBC's Brian Williams tried to bait Ryan into a "war on women" dialogue by asking how the party's positions on abortion would play among suburban women. Ryan redi-

## Liberal Abortion Laws Hurt Poor Women of Color

Only California can match New York in ramping up abortion rights. . . .

As always, no one suffers more from liberalized abortion laws than minorities. . . . This is nothing new. In 2008, a chain of abortion clinics in Southern California had at least six doctors on staff with histories of medical malpractice, and most of their clients were low-income Latinas. In New York State the abortion rate is double the national average, and in New York City the rate for black women exceeds 60 percent. This phenomenon is not by accident—it is the result of public policy.

*Bill Donohue, Newsmax, March 20, 2013.*
*www.newsmax.com*

rected, responding: "You know, I think what suburban women are mostly worried about is jobs. I mean, look who got hit hardest in this economy. It's women. Poverty among women is at a 17-year high. . . . So, that's what most women are asking us about." And in his prime-time convention speech, the "women's issue" Romney highlighted was the threat of tax hikes faced by female entrepreneurs.

Romney and Ryan need to keep making this case, because it is a powerful one. Obama's record, after all, is clear. The president's vision of "women's empowerment" is economic stagnation and welfare-state dependency, papered over with platitudes about abortions that many women don't want and government-subsidized contraception many women don't need.

What women really need is jobs. They need opportunities to apply their education and their talents.

They want to be rewarded justly for hard work, not to see the fruits of their labor confiscated by a government that refuses to deal with irresponsible deficits and debt. They want to choose their own doctors, and want access to good health care for themselves and their children. They want their marriages to be happy and stable, and their churches free and thriving. It's impossible to poll unborn girls, of course, but presumably they'd like to live. On the whole, women want to be taken seriously as voters. They want to be free and equal citizens—not wards of the state.

Romney and Ryan need to speak to these concerns and show how Republican policies will advance these aims. President Obama surely won't. After four years, he has nothing to show for himself—hence the great deception of the "war on women."

> "Republicans have initiated a calculated assault on women . . . and Democrats . . . have, too often, failed to step up when the party's most reliable constituency are up against the wall."

# Both Parties Use Divisive Views on Women's Health Issues to Distract Voters

*Renee Parsons*

*Renee Parsons is a former staffer in the US House of Representatives and a lobbyist for Friends of the Earth, an environmental organization. She is a member of the board of the Treasure Coast branch of the American Civil Liberties Union, and a frequent contributor to various progressive blogs and publications. In the following viewpoint, she contends that conservative Republicans are waging a full-scale war on women's reproductive freedom and are seemingly unaware that in doing so they are directly opposing the due process clause of the Constitution's Fourteenth Amendment, the basis for the 1973* Roe v. Wade *Supreme Court decision legalizing abortion. Republicans, she argues, are advancing increasingly regressive women's health poli-*

cies to garner the support of pro-life voters, even when doing so goes against their stated positions on Americans' constitutional right to privacy and on limiting government intervention. Democratic politicians are also at fault, Parsons maintains, because not only have they failed to effectively oppose Republicans' efforts to limit women's freedom of choice, they have often supported antichoice legislation to gain votes. Both parties, she concludes, are using women's health as a political football.

As you read, consider the following questions:

1. Who was the only Republican senator to vote against the Blunt Amendment, according to Parsons?

2. With what chromosomal abnormality was Rick Santorum's daughter afflicted, as reported by the author?

3. According to Parsons, what year was the Hyde Amendment adopted?

After months of Republican presidential candidates embarrassing themselves and the party of Abraham Lincoln and Theodore Roosevelt with religious zealotry dominating the [2012] primary season, the relentless assault on a woman's health care choices can be expected to continue as it distracts American voters from an authentic debate on other important issues that dominate American life today.

More than just a divinely-inspired reverence for life, the coordinated war on women has whipped the ideologically-pure Republican base to a fine froth that has added a gender gap to the national campaign and alienated registered Independent female voters, 48 percent of whom are now siding with the Democrats.

At the center of the anti-choice movement is a testosterone-driven opposition, the majority of whom will never find themselves pregnant yet believe they are imbued with the right to impose their religious beliefs on a woman's most intimate life decision and on a woman who does not share their views.

## A Lack of Due Process

Social conservatives have conveniently lost sight of the fact that *Roe v. Wade* was based on the Constitution's Fourteenth Amendment 'due process' clause guaranteeing each individual a right to privacy, free from unwarranted government intrusion and that Constitutional protection for the use of contraceptives was affirmed by the Supreme Court in 1965. While a direct attack on the Fourteenth Amendment is fraught with unintended consequences, anti-choice activists have shrewdly chosen to broaden their efforts against health needs for women in open disdain.

It does seem incredulous that Republican candidates, full of righteous pontifications have handed the largest, most important voting bloc to the Democrats as it escalates its ongoing war on women. The Republican party's attack not only jeopardizes the national Republican party's credibility but is in evidence in state legislatures across the country that have been on the march to deny women their Constitutionally-protected rights [to abortion].

Most recently, Sen. Roy Blunt's (R-MO) harsh amendment to allow an employer to deny reproductive health services to women based on moral or religious principles failed on a too-close-for-comfort 51-48 vote with only one Republican, retiring Sen. Olympia Snowe (R-ME) voting with the Democrats and three Democrats including Sen. Bob Casey (D-PA) voting with the Republicans.

Yet, in Massachusetts, Sen. Scott Brown's (R-MA) vote in support of the Blunt amendment was a sign of the church's political power and indicative of recent polls showing him with an eight point lead over Harvard law professor Elizabeth Warren, a clear supporter of women's health issues.

## Positions of Presidential Hopefuls

Blunt's amendment could have been a heaven sent opportunity for Mitt Romney, who appears as stiff as Al Gore in 2000, to begin to pivot as a 'moderate' Republican—a dying breed to be sure. Romney's first reaction was one that you might expect from a former Governor of liberal Massachusetts when he said that ". . . the idea of presidential candidates getting into questions about contraception within a relationship between a man and a woman, husband and wife, I'm not going there," and then later, "Contraception is working just fine, let's just leave it alone." Within hours, however, the timid Romney backtracked in support of Blunt proving that he will do whatever it takes to be elected.

Enter former Pennsylvania Sen. Rick Santorum surrounded by "Catholic Homeschoolers for Santorum" signs who attacked Romney for lacking conservative instincts on social issues like contraception which Santorum referred to as a "'license' to do things 'in the sexual realm.'"

In addition to opposing abortion with no exceptions even in the case of rape or incest, Santorum has given every reason to believe that his policies on women's health issues are so narrow and regressive as to take the country back to the 19th Century. Even as Santorum and his wife, a former nurse, experienced the tragedy of a daughter born with Trisomy 18, a chromosomal abnormality with a low rate of survival, the couple made the painful decision to refuse a doctor's recommendation to abort. Yet he remains opposed to prenatal testing for a damaged fetus.

Given Newt Gingrich's well-known history with women, his pledge to support anti-choice appointments and the prosecution of doctors who provide abortions is in sync with his otherwise callow, crude candidacy. Ron Paul, who has yet to win a primary, once supported, as a true libertarian, a woman's right to choose but is now in the 'life begins at conception' column.

## Democrats Have a Mixed Bag

Meanwhile, Barack Obama has embraced the women's health issue as the Democratic party's commitment has surpassed the Republicans but, over the years, has been a mixed bag when the chips are down.

Even as Congressional Democrats protected Planned Parenthood from a Republican assault in 2011, Democrats have historically provided the margin to reauthorize the Hyde Amendment each year. Adopted in 1976, the once controversial amendment which bans abortions for Medicaid recipients is not a permanent law but a 'rider' which requires annual reauthorization. Yet, even when Democrats have controlled both houses of Congress, the amendment makes its way silently through the legislative labyrinth to passage without benefit of a public hearing, witnesses or medical testimony.

During early debate on the Affordable Care Act of 2009, the president threatened to veto the Act if it did not include abortion funding and yet ultimately accepted the status quo of no Federal funds for abortion. In a separate action, Democrats joined Republicans in banning D.C.-funded abortions for poor women.

As critically important as women's health concerns are to many American women who struggle with the country's meager health care coverage, both political parties need to be held accountable as beltway [Washington, DC] Republicans have initiated a calculated assault on women in the name of religious freedom and Democrats who talk a good race as they woo female votes have, too often, failed to step up when the party's most reliable constituency are up against the wall.

With legal abortions widely available throughout Europe, including predominately Catholic Spain, Germany, France and Italy, it is curious that abortion policy in the U.S. remains stuck in the 1800s as a political hot-button issue—even after *Roe v. Wade* presumably settled the issue.

Powerful adversaries like the U.S. Conference of Catholic Bishops who would benefit from a better understanding of the First Amendment's separation of church and state, have promised to overturn the new contraceptive coverage rules, and will be joined by the extreme right wing to form a potent

*"Stripping Planned Parenthood of federal funding would . . . sacrifice the 97 percent of its public health work that has nothing to do with abortion, from which many people benefit directly."*

# Political Attacks on Planned Parenthood Are a Threat to Women's Health

**Scientific American**

Scientific American *was founded in 1845 and covers issues of scientific and technological interest. In the following viewpoint, the magazine argues that Republican efforts to end federal funding for Planned Parenthood, a major public and reproductive health institution, would have grave implications for women's health. The author explains that 97 percent of Planned Parenthood's services are essential for low-income women, who have no other access to preventive health services such as mammograms and Pap tests. Republican lawmakers' claims that Planned Parenthood's primary function is to perform abortions, Scientific American declares, are false. In fact, only 3 percent of Planned Parenthood's resources are devoted to abortion services,*

*and no federal funds are used to cover these services. By provid-*
*ing women with access to contraception and family planning, the*
*authors conclude, Planned Parenthood has played a vital role in*
*enhancing and preserving the health and well-being of US*
*women. Defunding Planned Parenthood, the authors contend,*
*would devastate the country.*

As you read, consider the following questions:

1. How much is Planned Parenthood's annual budget, according to *Scientific American*?

2. According to the authors, what year did Planned Parenthood begin providing abortion services?

3. What percentage of births were unwanted in 2002, according to the authors?

Almost 100 years ago Margaret Sanger opened a tiny birth-
control clinic in the Brownsville section of Brooklyn, N.Y.
Poor Yiddish- and Italian-speaking women, overwhelmed by
large families that they could not support, would come for ad-
vice about how to avoid pregnancy and the dangers of hor-
rific, sometimes life-threatening, self-administered abortions.
The clinic taught women to use the diaphragm. Nine days after it opened, Sanger and two other women who ran the center were jailed for violating a New York State law that prohibited contraception.

This clinic eventually grew into Planned Parenthood, the
nation's largest nonprofit supplier of reproductive health services to women and men. A century after its founding, the organization is again at the heart of one of the most divisive issues in American political life. It has come under attack by
Republican presidential candidates seeking to revoke the
group's federal funding—almost half of its $1-billion budget
comes from federal and state sources. Last year the House of
Representatives voted to withdraw some of its support, although the measure was not sustained in the Senate.

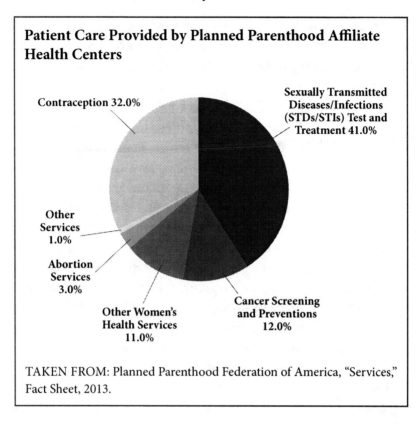

**Patient Care Provided by Planned Parenthood Affiliate Health Centers**

Contraception 32.0%

Sexually Transmitted Diseases/Infections (STDs/STIs) Test and Treatment 41.0%

Other Services 1.0%

Abortion Services 3.0%

Other Women's Health Services 11.0%

Cancer Screening and Preventions 12.0%

TAKEN FROM: Planned Parenthood Federation of America, "Services," Fact Sheet, 2013.

(Backing for the group, initiated under the Nixon administration, has not always been a partisan issue.) In March, Mitt Romney, the GOP's presumptive presidential candidate, vowed to end federal funding if elected. This is a worrying prospect for both women and public health.

For some people, Planned Parenthood has come to symbolize abortion, which it has provided since 1970. But in all the rhetoric, facts have sometimes gone missing. For instance, Senator Jon Kyl of Arizona declared last year on the floor of the Senate that abortion accounts for "well over 90 percent" of what Planned Parenthood does. The actual figure is 3 percent. (Planned Parenthood clinics perform one in four abortions in the U.S. but use no federal funds for this practice.) To some abortion opponents, that 3 percent is reason enough to gut the organization. If a future Congress and White House were to do so, however, it would drive women once again into the back alleys, without necessarily decreasing the number of abortions.

Stripping Planned Parenthood of federal funding would also sacrifice the 97 percent of its public health work that has nothing to do with abortion, from which many people benefit directly. One in five American women have used the group's services, and three out of four of its patients are considered to have low incomes. In 2011 it carried out tests and treatment for more than four million individuals with sexually transmitted diseases. It supplied 750,000 exams to prevent breast cancer, the most common cancer among U.S. women. And it performed 770,000 Pap tests to prevent cervical cancer, which was a leading cause of death among women before this screen became widely available. Planned Parenthood is one of the most important public health care institutions in the country, even aside from its work in rational family planning.

Family planning has benefited society in numerous ways. It has saved lives, opened new horizons for women and kept populations from soaring. Since 1965, the year the Supreme Court struck down a Connecticut law that made access to contraception illegal, women's ability to plan and space out pregnancies has contributed to a 60 percent decline in maternal deaths. By 2002, moreover, only 9 percent of births were unwanted, compared with 20 percent in the early 1960s. As a major provider of contraceptives—it furnished birth control to two million Americans last year—Planned Parenthood serves as "America's largest abortion preventer," as one *Chicago Tribune* writer pointed out.

Access to birth control in the U.S. has helped narrow the income inequality gap between men and women by as much as 30 percent during the 1990s alone. The pill has given women greater choice about when to have children, freeing them up to acquire career skills. By 2009 women procured more than half of all U.S. doctoral degrees, compared with 10 percent in 1960. The health and well-being of a society correlates highly with the status of its women. In many parts of the Middle East, Asia and Africa, women are now making gains, to the betterment of all, in access to education and jobs—both contingent on family planning. Now is a particularly bad time for Americans, as citizens of the world, to forget what we have accomplished at home.

> "Planned Parenthood's blatant misuse of taxpayer dollars to fund its big abortion business is an attack on life and women's health. . . . It must be stopped."

# Planned Parenthood: Making a Killing

*Tony Perkins*

*Tony Perkins is the president of the Family Research Council, a conservative Judeo-Christian-oriented public policy organization. In the following viewpoint, Perkins argues that Americans should be outraged that over a half-billion US tax dollars were given the Planned Parenthood Federation of America, Inc., in fiscal year 2011–2012, even though the group reported $155 million in profits for that same period. While government support for Planned Parenthood has increased 167 percent over the last decade, Perkins argues, the group's cancer screening and contraceptive services have decreased, and despite claims to the contrary, Planned Parenthood has never performed mammograms. Meanwhile, he contends, thousands of children and women have been killed by abortions at Planned Parenthood clinics. To protect women and children and save US taxpayers money, Perkins concludes, the Title X Abortion Provider Prohibition Act, legislation* *prohibiting the granting of Title X federal monies for organizations performing abortions, must be passed. Furthermore, Perkins adds, Republican leaders should refuse to raise the federal borrowing limit unless Planned Parenthood is defunded.*

As you read, consider the following questions:

1. How much does Perkins say Planned Parenthood received from federal, state, and local governments in 2012?

2. By what percentage did cancer screenings at Planned Parenthood decrease, according to Perkins?

3. Which US lawmaker is sponsoring the Title X Abortion-Provider Prohibition Act, as reported by the author?

It's been 1,350 days since the Senate passed a budget, but the checks to Planned Parenthood keep flowing! While American companies suffer, business at Cecile Richards's group couldn't be better. According to the organization's latest annual report (FY 2011–12), it looks like the government helped Planned Parenthood to another record year. For the second time in as many years, Richards's "nonprofit" is celebrating more than a billion dollars in total revenue—and almost half of it came courtesy of U.S. taxpayers.

America's abortion provider managed to squeeze $542.4 million out of federal, state, and local governments last year—a $55 million bump from 2010. And judging by its $155 million profit, the organization hardly needed the money! Still, Congress insists on being Planned Parenthood's biggest benefactor—even if it means borrowing millions from China to pay for it. The government chipped in the lion's share of Richards's budget (45%) last year, and then raised taxes on us to keep the killing machine afloat. That should outrage every American, regardless of how they feel about abortion. The President complains about tax breaks for millionaires—while he supports welfare for billionaire organizations!

## It's Time to Stop All Government Funding to Planned Parenthood

Planned Parenthood is neither building its non-abortion clientele nor expanding its services. Instead, it is concentrating on growing its abortion business and improving its profit margin, while abusing children with its "comprehensive sex education." Posing as a healthcare organization, it garners obscene amounts of taxpayer money to pay extremely high salaries to its top CEOs, while pocketing over 1.2 billion dollars in profits since 1966 and corrupting untold millions of children with its sex indoctrination programs.

*Rita Diller, LifeNews.com,*
*January 17, 2013.*

Fox News crunched the numbers and was shocked to find that government support for Planned Parenthood had jumped by 167% in the last 10 years alone. Of course, as more states aggressively step in to defund Planned Parenthood, the Left has been just as aggressive in filling the gap. They claim the money helps women, but based on this report, Planned Parenthood was too busy reelecting President Obama to help anyone! Cancer screenings (the theme of Richards's incessant election ads) dropped by a stunning 29% in 2011–12, and contraception services slumped 12%. Of course, the number of mammograms performed at Planned Parenthood stayed the same: zero.

While all of this "vital medical care" plunged, the group's primary moneymaker—abortion—raked in more than ever. It was one of the bloodiest years in the organization's history, as unborn casualties climbed to 333,964—enough to fill Yankee stadium six and a half times. The loss of life represented a

4,519 spike in abortions (almost twice the enrollment of Regent University). In just three years, Richards's group has claimed credit for 995,687 deaths through abortion—and that doesn't include the handful of women lost to botched abortions in the last 12 months. Perhaps the biggest misnomer about the organization is this: most people aren't planning parenthood when they visit these clinics; they're planning abortions. That was obvious from the tiny sliver of adoption referrals from Richards's network: 2,300—barely one half of one percent of the total abortions performed.

Meanwhile, the organization credited their success to the "generosity of several key donors and funders"—which, if Rep. Diane Black (R-Tenn.) gets her way, will no longer include the U.S. Congress. Her bill, the Title X Abortion Provider Prohibition Act (H.R. 217), would pull the financial rug out of Planned Parenthood where its "family planning" dollars are concerned. If successful, the legislation she introduced Friday would zero out Title X money for any group that performs or refers for abortion. A nurse for more than 40 years, Rep. Black knows a little something about health care—and abortion, which hurts women *and* children, isn't it. "Planned Parenthood's blatant misuse of taxpayer dollars to fund its big abortion business is an attack on life and women's health," she said in a statement. "It must be stopped."

Now that the country has maxed out its credit cards, the House is preparing to do battle over the debt ceiling. If Richards's group alone is blowing a half-billion dollar hole in our debt, here's a suggestion for GOP leaders. Make defunding Planned Parenthood a condition of raising the federal borrowing limit. What do conservatives have to lose—except millions of future taxpayers if this madness doesn't stop?

> *"Planned Parenthood has to understand that when they fund both non-controversial healthcare services and controversial services, that the non-controversial services will suffer funding cuts."*

# Planned Parenthood's Stance on Abortion Makes Its Preventive Services Vulnerable to Political Pressure

*Dominic A. Carone*

*Dominic A. Carone is a neuropsychologist and an associate professor at the State University of New York's Upstate University Hospital. In the following viewpoint, Carone argues that because Planned Parenthood provides abortion services and supports pro-choice legislation, it risks losing support for its important health care services, such as mammograms. Carone explains that the competing political interests of groups such as Susan G. Komen for the Cure (a breast cancer research funding organization), which has connections to various key Republican legislators, and Planned Parenthood, which has connections to powerful Demo-*

*crats, are bound to interfere with the Planned Parenthood's health care services, especially when the group takes a stand on controversial issues like abortion. Carone concludes that Susan G. Komen's decision to first withdraw and then restore funding to Planned Parenthood—both in response to political pressure—demonstrates how vulnerable to politics women's health care services are.*

As you read, consider the following questions:

1. How many abortions does Carone say Planned Parenthood performs each year?

2. For what US president did Nancy Brinker serve as ambassador, according to the author?

3. According to Carone, what company funds the Susan G. Komen organization?

Despite the adversarial political climate that divides so many Americans, there are some topics that most people can agree on regardless of politics. One of those is that early detection and screening for cervical cancer and breast cancer are important initiatives that should be supported because early detection leads to earlier treatment which, in turn, saves lives. While many women have such exams paid for by their health care insurance, those without insurance often rely on funding from non-profit organizations to fund these types of early clinical, screening, and diagnostic exams.

Problems emerge, however, when one of these health care organizations takes a position on a topic as controversial as abortion, either pro or con. For example, Planned Parenthood is a non-profit organization that relies heavily on donors to fund women's healthcare services, which includes clinical breast exams and mammograms. However, the organization also conducts about 300,000 abortions a year and lobbies for pro-abortion legislation. In doing so, Planned Parenthood intertwines funding for activities that almost everyone would support (breast exams) with funding for an activity (abortions) that deeply divides Americans.

## Susan G. Komen and Political Pressure

When this happens, such an organization can expect to be the target of people who have strong opposing views on abortion. This is exactly what has happened to Planned Parenthood, as they have been frequently audited and targeted for defunding by Congressional Republicans. Most recently, the largest breast cancer organization in the U.S. (Susan G. Komen for the Cure) decided to cut its funding to Planned Parenthood. Although the money donated from Susan G. Komen was for clinical breast exams and mammograms, Republicans criticized the group for supporting a group that supported abortions. Susan G. Komen claimed that the reason for their decision was because they had developed a new rule prohibiting donations to organizations that are under congressional investigation. However, critics claim that this is a contrived excuse, especially since it only affected funding of Planned Parenthood.

Delving into the politics of this issue in more detail gives reason to suspect that this was a contrived excuse by Susan G. Komen when the real issue involved giving into political and financial pressures. Specifically, the founder of Susan G. Komen is Nancy Brinker, who has long-standing connections to the Republican party, served as an Ambassador for George W. Bush, donating money to the Republican party (including George W. Bush's first presidential campaign), and partnered with the policy-making branch of the George W. Bush presidential library. In fact, the decision to cut off funding to Planned Parenthood was made soon after the latter partnership was established.

To make the situation even more politically interesting, the leader of Planned Parenthood is Cecile Richards, who was the daughter of former Texas Democratic governor, Anne Richards. Richards is widely remembered for ridiculing George W.

Bush when he ran against her for governor. Thus, it is not much a stretch to imagine that a condition for partnership with Susan. G. Komen (which is worth 3 million dollars and is funded by [pharmaceuticals giant] Merck, a known campaign donor to current Texas governor, Rick Perry) could have been dependent on defunding Planned Parenthood. Susan G. Komen has denied that their decision has anything to do with politics, which is hard to believe, and this brings me to my last point.

## At the Mercy of Politics

If Susan G. Komen truly wanted to defund Planned Parenthood because they did not want to support a group that also funded abortions, that is well within their right to do. Planned Parenthood has to understand that when they fund both non-controversial healthcare services and controversial services, that the non-controversial services will suffer funding cuts from organizations who are pressured to stop contributing to them. Separating these services into different groups would at least prevent this problem from occurring, regardless of one's position on abortion. In cases where funding is cut off, it is misleading to paint the organization that cuts the funding as creating barriers to women's health because the problem would not exist if Planned Parenthood did not simultaneously fund controversial and non-controversial health services. They are within their right to do so, but it will cause problems as a result.

At the same time, it is not a mystery that Planned Parenthood pays for abortions. Thus, if another organization is truly opposed to abortions, they should simply not make a contribution in the first place. Once an organization makes a contribution and then stops contributing after known pressure and associations with opponents of Planned Parenthood, the decision is going to appear politically and financially motivated even if by some chance it was not.

# Periodical and Internet Sources Bibliography

*The following articles have been selected to supplement the diverse views presented in this chapter.*

| Kirsten Andersen | "US Democrats Target Crisis Pregnancy Centers with New Bill," LifeSiteNews, May 21, 2013. www.lifesitenews.com. |
| Gretchen Borchelt | "State Politicians Continue to Play Politics with Women's Health, Threatening a Woman's Right to Abortion," *National Women's Law Center Blog*, October 17, 2013. www.nwlc.org. |
| Katie Cole | "HPV Vaccine: Valuing Health over Politics," American Association of University Women, July 3, 2013. www.aauw.org. |
| Tara Culp-Ressler | "How Abortion Stigma Impacts Our Politics," ThinkProgress, May 1, 2013. http://thinkprogress.org. |
| Jonah Goldberg | "Abortion Rights Not Synonymous with Women's Health," Townhall, June 28, 2013. http://townhall.com. |
| Dahlia Lithwick | "Finally! Anti-choice Activists Have Been Gunning Hard to Outlaw Abortion. Today, the Democrats Pushed Back," *Slate*, November 13, 2013. www.slate.com. |
| Jeanne Monahan | "The *Washington Post*'s Disservice to Women," *National Review*, September 6, 2013. |
| Jacqueline Murphy | "Anti-women's Health Politicians Continue to Fight Losing Battles in Court," Planned Parenthood, August 21, 2013. www.plannedparenthoodaction.org. |
| John Sides and Lynn Vavreck | "Republicans Haven't Lost Women," Bloomberg, November 7, 2013. www.bloomberg.com. |

OPPOSING
VIEWPOINTS®
SERIES

CHAPTER 2

# What Should Be the Role of Religion in Women's Health Care Policy?

# Chapter Preface

As the American Muslim population steadily increases, US doctors and other health care providers are learning how to deal sensitively with the unique religious and cultural needs of Muslim women. During the last few years several outreach efforts have been launched to raise awareness among health care providers of the beliefs and practices of Muslim women and the best ways to respect them while also providing them with the highest quality care. Because physical modesty is paramount to Muslim women, many of whom cover their heads at all times and uncover certain parts of their body only when in the presence of family members, many will only permit physical examinations by a female physician or nurse practitioner and may insist upon being examined only through a gown. Many American Muslim women avoid seeking preventive care out of a desire to protect their modesty and because they cannot find a female practitioner. Dr. Aasim I. Padela, an emergency room physician at the University of Michigan Hospital and author of a paper published in the *Journal of Medical Ethics* on Muslim patients in the health care system, recalls the experience of a Muslim woman who underwent surgery: "She went to a physician whom she trusted and told him, 'I need to at least have my head covering on when I leave the operating room.' When she woke up, she was wearing a gown, but her head was uncovered. She was livid. She had been there many hours. She will never go back to that hospital again."

Padela explains that while it may not always be possible to make exceptions for or to accommodate such religious restrictions as no touching between unrelated members of the opposite sex, there are ways that male physicians can make such women more comfortable, such as by wearing gloves to avoid direct skin contact, by allowing the women to wear their own clothing or providing them with modest gowns for examination and hospitalization, by having a female nurse practitioner examine them while the physician observes, or often simply by acknowledging that they may be uncomfortable and asking how the doctor can help make them more comfortable. While some doctors feel that they do not have time to ask additional questions or accommodate religious or cultural traditions and beliefs, many agree with Dr. Hasan Shanawani, who belongs to the Islamic Medical Association of North America's ethics committee and is an assistant professor of Internal Medicine at Wayne State University and a physician at the John D. Dingell VA Medical Center in Detroit. Shanawani maintains that "the onus is on you the doctor to make sure that your patients' modesty and personal dignity are being protected."

Muslim women's religious and cultural needs are just one aspect of how religion impacts women's health care. In the following chapter, authors debate the role that religion does and should or should not play in determining government policy surrounding such aspects of women's health care as insurance coverage for birth control, and whether conscience-protection clauses protect or violate religious freedom.

> "I do not think that there can be much
> doubt that requiring a religious institu-
> tion to pay for services that it regards
> as immoral or evil is a burden on the
> exercise of religion."

# Religion Has a Legitimate Role in Decisions About Women's Health Care Policies

*Michael McConnell*

*Michael McConnell is the Richard and Frances Mallery Professor of Law at Stanford University. In the following viewpoint, taken from his remarks at the Georgetown Symposium on Religious Freedom and Healthcare Reform in March 2012, McConnell argues that the US Department of Health and Human Services mandate for birth control coverage violates the Constitution's First Amendment and the Religious Freedom Restoration Act. Requiring religious institutions to provide funding for services it regards as immoral or evil has never been the practice of the federal government, McConnell contends. Rather, the tradition has been to allow exceptions on the basis of religion. He asserts that*

Michael McConnell, "Report of the Georgetown Symposium on Religious Freedom and Healthcare Reform," Religious Freedom Project, Berkley Center for Religion, Peace, and World Affairs, Georgetown University, March 22, 2012, pp. 8–10. Copyright © 2012 by Berkley Center for Religion, Peace, and World Affairs. All rights reserved. Reproduced by permission.

*the compromise offered by President Barack Obama that employees of religious institutions could indirectly obtain coverage does not stand up to economic or legal scrutiny. No government interest, he concludes, makes it necessary to force religious institutions to offer women contraception.*

As you read, consider the following questions:

1. In what year was the Religious Freedom Restoration Act passed, according to the author?

2. What does McConnell see as a possible justification for exceptions for contraceptive coverage and co-pays?

3. In what year during the Bill Clinton administration was a version of the health care bill including a very broad religious accommodation passed, according to McConnell?

I am not a Roman Catholic and I do not share the Church's theology with respect to contraception. I am here because of my interest and commitment to religious liberty. To my mind the issue here is not related to the specifics of the mandate,[1] but rather to the unprecedented decision to require not only religious institutions but also other Americans to pay for something that they regard as deeply contrary to their beliefs.

There are two bodies of law that are applicable to this question: statutory and constitutional. The main statutory constraint here is the Religious Freedom Restoration Act, which was passed in 1993, and signed by President [Bill] Clinton. That law stipulates that whenever actions of the federal government impose a substantial burden on the exercise of religion, they can be sustained only if they are the least restrictive means of achieving a compelling governmental interest.

---

1. The "HHS mandate," a provision of the Patient Protection and Affordable Care Act of 2010 that requires all employers, including religious organizations, to provide insurance coverage of contraception and sterilization.

Firstly, is this regulation a substantial burden on the exercise of religion? And secondly, is it a narrowly tailored means of serving an important governmental purpose? In addition to that, there are the free exercise and establishment clauses of the First Amendment, which are guarantees of religious freedom. Just a few months ago [in January 2012] the United States Supreme Court rendered a remarkably powerful, unanimous decision in *Hosanna-Tabor v. EEOC* [Equal Employment Opportunity Commission] re-emphasizing the protection that religious institutions have for being able to make decisions important to their beliefs and their mission. It was a unanimous decision, I might add, rejecting the argument of the Justice Department and this [Obama] administration, that the free exercise and establishment clause provided no special protection to religious institutions at all. Interestingly, even Justice [Elena] Kagan, who had been the solicitor general [the official who argues for the government before the Supreme Court] not that long ago, joined in an opinion emphatically rejecting that argument, calling it "remarkable", which is judge-speak for "really out of line." I wonder if this contraceptive mandate is not a product of the same kind of legal thinking that went into the Justice Department's brief.

## A Burden on the Exercise of Religion

Let me begin first with the burden. I do not think that there can be much doubt that requiring a religious institution to pay for services that it regards as immoral or evil is a burden on the exercise of religion. That seems to me to be rather obvious but let me give an analogy. I have no doubt that the federal government can make contraceptive services and sterilization and abortifacients available, as a matter of federal policy. The analogy here is to making war. I have no doubt that the federal government has a right to have a military establishment and to make war. It can use tax money that comes into the general treasury to do that, even though many Americans have a religious and sometimes non-religious moral objection to warfare. What the federal government cannot do is require religious institutions or conscientiously objecting individual citizens to make war for them. They cannot conscript the churches of America into assisting in the war effort. Throughout American history, we have always provided exemptions for religious conscientious objectors in this regard.

Similarly, it is not that there is any restriction on the federal government in pursuing its particular understanding of healthcare services in America. It is that they cannot conscript religious institutions and individuals into carrying out that program for them. I think that the [Obama] administration's policy actually acknowledges that that is so. Because, from the beginning and even before the controversy, the administration exempted some religious institutions precisely on the ground that they did understand that this would be a burden on their religious conscience. However, it only exempted those religious institutions that primarily serve members of the same religion. They initially called this a "houses of worship" exception, as if churches in America did not do things like run soup kitchens, adoption services, international aid relief, aid for the poor, hospitals, schools and so forth. It is as if churches were only places where people retreat on Sunday mornings in order to talk among themselves. If you leaf through some of the rhetoric that comes from the administration on the subject, they actually very rarely refer to the exercise of religion. They speak instead of the freedom to worship, as if religion is just about worship rather than serving God in all the manifest ways in which religious institutions do so.

## President Obama's Compromise

After the commotion, and under a great deal of political heat, the president announced that there would be a so-called compromise. First of all, we have not yet seen the compromise. The present rule is a final rule and it is in effect. There is a proposed rule-making which does nothing other than make a suggestion and ask people to make comments on how we can possibly provide free services of this sort to employees of religious institutions without anybody having to pay for it. My guess is that Economics 101 will kick in at some point and they will realize that is not a possible proposition. In the meantime, we have regulations that are final and in place, requiring religious institutions to submit.

Let us think about the compromise for just a moment. As I understand it, the idea is that the healthcare policies that religious institutions provide will not themselves have to cover the objectionable services, but individuals who are covered can call the insurance company and add an additional rider to that policy. It is only by virtue of being covered by that policy that they have the right to do this. They get to add to that policy these additional services at no cost. Now I submit to you that that is no different in substance whatsoever because the policies still cover everything that the individuals are entitled to. I would say it is a fig leaf, but I think that this proposal actually gives fig leaves a bad name. It is sometimes said that the way this works is that providing these preventive services will actually save the insurance companies money and therefore they really do not need to charge for them. I think that that is a rather bizarre economic argument. If that were so, then we would not have to have a contraceptive mandate anyway because profit-making insurance companies, wanting to save money, would be handing out contraceptives for free without anybody telling them to.

Take, for example, other prescription drugs, for which co-payments are required under most healthcare plans. For some reason the administration believes that there should be an exception for contraceptive drugs and no copayments. I can see no justification for that other than possibly a giveaway to drug companies, who will be able to profit from that. For example, I take blood pressure medication. But do they give it to me for free? It would save them money because the blood pressure medicine is cheaper than the heart attack that I might very well have. But no, they do not give that to me for free. The money for contraceptive coverage is going to come from somewhere and the only place that it will come from is the premium that is paid for the coverage. So it seems to me quite clear that even with the so-called compromise, this proposal places a substantial burden on the religious institutions.

## The Governmental Interest

Let us then ask what the governmental interest is. It seems to me quite clear that all of this is about cost shifting. Instead of the government itself providing the service it thinks is important, it is trying to shift the cost onto employers, including religious employers, which is not a compelling governmental interest at all. But in law, how do we make the judgment as to when interests are compelling? It is a very sort of political, subjective question. We ask whether other institutions in similar circumstances insist upon the same thing because if something is truly compelling, then in other analogous circumstances, the government is going to be taking the same view.

First of all, many states already have contraceptive mandates, but none of them impose them in the same sweeping, exception-less way that this proposal does. Most of them allow religious employers to self-insure and thereby not provide the contraceptive coverage. If you look at past proposals, when [then First Lady] Hillary Clinton tried to work toward a similar health program back in the Clinton administration, the version of that bill that passed the Senate Finance Committee included a very broad religious accommodation. If it was okay back in 1994 in the Clinton Administration, I do not know why it is not permissible or a reasonable accommodation today. And in fact, if you look at the whole panoply of federal healthcare laws, to my knowledge every one of them that potentially might infringe upon religious conscience has an exception.

What is more, even this rule has exceptions that affect millions of people. If it were a compelling governmental interest to make sure that every employee gets this kind of coverage, there would not be, for example, the exceptions for houses of worship. There would not be the exceptions for grandfathered policies. Literally millions of Americans will still have the same coverage as before with no contraceptive mandate attached. If it is okay to exempt millions of people in order to comply with a political promise made by the president, I suggest to you it is okay to exempt religious institutions.

How else could the government achieve its goals? Under the Religious Freedom Restoration Act they have to use the least restrictive means of doing it. . . . Title 10 already provides low cost contraceptives to millions and millions of people. Let the government expand its programs if that is the purpose. But it should not require churches, for whom this is a moral evil, to do it for them.

> "The First Amendment's religious free-
> dom principles do not include the right
> to impose one's religious views on oth-
> ers."

# Religion Should Have No Role in Decisions About Women's Health Care Policies

*National Women's Law Center*

*The National Women's Law Center (NWLC) advocates the pas-
sage of laws and public policies in the US that support women's
rights in education, employment, family and economic security,
and health and reproductive rights, with a particular emphasis
on the needs of low-income women and their families. In the following viewpoint, a fact sheet produced by the NWLC, the center outlines various ways in which refusals of health care services
on religious grounds violate US women's constitutional right to
health care and reproductive freedom. The First Amendment, the
center claims, protects religious freedom but does not include
provisions allowing any individual or group to impose religious
beliefs on others, which is what hospitals and pharmacies that
deny reproductive health care to women on the basis of religion
are doing.*

As you read, consider the following questions:

1. How many times more likely are rural residents to live in a medically underserved area, according to the author?

2. In what year did Kentucky governor Steve Beshear refuse to approve a merger of several hospitals, according to the NWLC?

3. When is the free exercise clause triggered, in the author's opinion?

Reproductive justice demands that women be able to access and make informed decisions about their reproductive health care. Unfortunately, hospitals and pharmacies sometimes use their religious beliefs to justify denying women not only access to but also information about reproductive health care, including contraception, abortion, and in vitro fertilization. However, the religious freedom protections embodied in the First Amendment do not include the right to use religion to discriminate. While individual providers may refuse to provide a service based on personal religious objections, the pharmacies and hospitals that employ them may not discriminate against the women who seek healthcare at their facilities by denying them the appropriate standard of medical care. Such religious discrimination violates a woman's right to make informed decisions about her health care and her reproductive freedom.

## Women's Health Is Jeopardized

Hospitals and pharmacies that use religious beliefs to deny women needed care may jeopardize women's health and future fertility. Catholic-affiliated hospitals, for example, are governed by the Ethical and Religious Directives for Catholic Health Care Services (the Directives), which prohibit abortion and contraception, as well as in vitro fertilization. Therefore, women who go to a Catholic-affiliated hospital may not only be denied basic reproductive care but also may not even be informed of the full range of health care options available to them. For example, women seeking treatment for miscarriages and ectopic pregnancies at Catholic-affiliated hospitals have been denied the appropriate standard of care and placed in life- and health-threatening situations. Rape survivors seeking care at hospitals have been refused information about and access to emergency contraception (EC), denying them the ability to prevent pregnancy. Pharmacies sometimes also deny women access to birth control or EC.

Women denied needed services are forced to bear the burden of additional costs, delays, and health risks incurred by going elsewhere. Some women may even be prohibited from going elsewhere because their insurer prevents them from seeking care outside the plan. Religious refusals are particularly detrimental to women of color, low-income women, and rural women because many already face considerable barriers that impede their access to care. Low-income women and women of color are significantly more likely than other women to have trouble gaining access to medical care because of inflexible work schedules and difficulty arranging childcare or transportation. Rural women and women living without health care providers in their communities might have to travel long distances to obtain care. Rural residents are four times more likely to live in a medically underserved area. Providers practicing certain specialties, such as obstetrics/gynecology, are particularly lacking in rural areas; this often presents a major barrier for rural women who need reproductive health services. A woman and her family in a rural area, and even some urban areas, may need to travel for hours—sometimes by multiple modes of transportation—in order to reach a pharmacy that stocks contraceptives or an abortion provider. Thus, women of color, low-income women and rural women may have to marshal considerable resources to see a provider and

## Obamacare's Religious Exemptions Are a Bad Joke

The Obama administration has said that promoting public health and gender equality are compelling . . . interests. We concur! But how can the administration promote public health and gender equality if they also give power-tripping zealots the leverage to impose "moral" agendas that directly contradict those interests?

We need to start acting like adults and stop letting fringe beliefs dictate public health policy. Plan B and the IUD [intrauterine device] are not abortion pills, no one is force-feeding birth control down anyone's throat, and women who want contraception and gain access to it will not prompt the End of Days.

*Katie J.M. Baker, Jezebel, November 28, 2012.*
*http://jezebel.com.*

in the event of a refusal, may have a harder time getting to another provider to access needed care. Although religious refusals jeopardize all women's health, they have the greatest effect on women with the fewest resources and who face the most barriers in accessing care.

## Reproductive Justice and Religious Freedom

The First Amendment protects religious freedom, an individual's right to practice or not practice any religion and an individual's right to be free from religious coercion. First, the Establishment Clause mandates government neutrality in religious matters by stating that the government "shall make no law respecting an establishment of religion." Second, the Free Exercise Clause protects an individual's right to practice his or her faith by stating that the government "shall make no law . . . prohibiting the free exercise [of religion]." As envisioned by the founders of the Constitution and interpreted by the Supreme Court today, religious freedom also includes the right to be free from religion and does not include a right to impose one's religion on another. Yet hospitals and pharmacies that refuse to provide reproductive healthcare to women do impose their religion on others.

In fact, reproductive health advocates have successfully used the Establishment Clause to challenge hospitals engaging in religious discrimination. For example, in 2011, Kentucky Governor Steve Beshear refused to approve a merger among several hospitals, including the University of Louisville Medical Center, which could have required all the hospitals to operate under the Directives, citing Establishment Clause concerns. According to a report about the proposed merger by the state's Attorney General, approval of the transaction would have had "the impermissible effect of advancing religion by authorizing and requiring a public, state-owned hospital to be governed by the Catholic Church's religious directives." Similarly, local residents in Newport, Oregon were able to stop an operating agreement under which the only hospital in their area would have been operated in accordance with the Directives while continuing to receive significant public funding and be overseen by a public corporation.

Moreover, when religious hospitals, pharmacies, or employers are required to provide women reproductive services that meet the standard of care, they may claim the requirement violates their free exercise of religion. However, the Free Exercise Clause is only triggered when a law intentionally targets a religion—it is not implicated by a neutral law of general applicability, like a law that regulates all hospitals or all employers. Neutral laws of general applicability are subject to minimal judicial scrutiny so that, as [US Supreme Court] Justice [Antonin] Scalia has stated, "each conscience" does not become "a law unto itself." For these reasons, the highest state courts in California and New York upheld those states' contraceptive coverage laws against challenges by Catholic-affiliated organizations claiming that the laws, which required them to provide insurance coverage for contraceptives because their employee health plans provided otherwise comprehensive prescription drug coverage, violated their religious freedom.

In both instances, the courts held that the laws furthered the compelling state interest of preventing gender discrimination and were neutral and generally applicable. Thus, the laws were allowed under the First Amendment.

## Women Must Have Full Access to Care

The First Amendment's religious freedom principles do not include the right to impose one's religious views on others. In order to make healthy decisions about their bodies, women must have access to all of their options when they seek medical care. Hospitals and pharmacies that refuse women needed reproductive care because of their religious beliefs are using their religion to discriminate against and harm others. This denies women the right to make informed decisions about their care and unnecessarily jeopardizes their health.

| "*Contraceptive use by women of all faiths is the overwhelming norm in US society.*"

# Contraceptive Coverage Protects Women's Health

*Guttmacher Institute*

*The Patient Protection and Affordable Care Act issued as an executive order by President Barack Obama in 2010 ensures that most private insurance plans provided by for-profit businesses will include contraceptive coverage. Some businesses have objected to providing contraception on religious grounds, and lawsuits have reached the US Supreme Court. As the Court prepared to hear arguments in the case, the Guttmacher Institute issued a statement supporting the importance of insurer-provided contraception coverage for all women. On June 30, 2014, the Supreme Court ruled in a 5–4 decision that family-owned corporations cannot be required under the Affordable Care Act to pay for insurance coverage for contraception. The Guttmacher Institute works to advance the sexual and reproductive health of all people worldwide through research, policy analysis and public education.*

Guttmacher Institute, "US Supreme Court Takes Up Contraceptive Coverage Guarantee," November 26, 2013. www.guttmacher.org.

As you read, consider the following questions:

1. What does the Affordable Care Act (ACA) guarantee that most private indurance plans will provide?

2. What are some of the health, social, and economic benefits for women to obtain and use contraception, according to the Guttmacher Institute?

3. According to the Guttmacher Institute, what is sound public health policy in regards to contraception?

The U.S. Supreme Court today [November 26, 2013] agreed to decide whether the owners of for-profit companies can assert religious objections to deny their employees insurance coverage of contraceptive services and supplies in employer-sponsored health plans. The 2010 Affordable Care Act (ACA) guarantees that most private plans will have contraceptive coverage without cost-sharing for patients. Churches and other houses of worship are exempted from this requirement and an accommodation is in place for religious nonprofit organizations.

However, the administration has determined that private, for-profit businesses cannot claim to be religious employers and are not exempted from providing contraceptive coverage (the U.S. Senate affirmed this decision by rejecting a measure known as the Blunt amendment that would have granted for-profit corporations extensive "conscience" rights). The Court's decision, if it were to grant for-profit corporations an exemption from covering contraception, could have significant negative effects on affected employees and their dependents— interfering with their ability to reap the well-documented health, social and economic benefits of contraceptive use.

## Benefits of Contraceptive Use

- **Health benefits:** A significant body of evidence shows that contraception is basic preventive health care for women. Broadening access to contraceptives by eliminating the daunting barrier that cost poses to effective contraceptive use is a significant gain for women's health and the health of their families. Removing that barrier for women covered by private health plans not only makes it easier for them to use contraceptives generally, but also allows them to use the most effective methods, like the IUD, which they might not previously have been able to afford due to high upfront costs.

- **Social and economic benefits:** Women's ability to obtain and effectively use contraceptives and thereby delay and space childbearing is crucial to their societal and economic advancement. Contraceptive use has a positive impact on women's education and workforce participation, as well as on subsequent outcomes related to their income, family stability, mental health and happiness, and the well-being of their children.

Women, of course, know about the myriad benefits of contraception from their own life experience. That's why virtually all women aged 15–44 who have ever had sexual intercourse have used at least one contraceptive method. However, consistent and correct contraceptive use is critical, which is why guaranteeing contraceptive coverage without co-pays for doctor's visits, patient information and counseling, and for whatever method works best for a woman—regardless of cost—has been such a crucial step forward for millions of U.S. women.

## Opposition to Contraception Is Not the Norm in US Society

Granting for-profit corporations the right to deny insurance coverage for contraceptive services interferes with the health of women and their families and their social and economic well-being. It would also allow these employers to effectively

## Health Care Refusals Undermine Quality Care

Health care is not like other fields. The delivery of health care is highly regulated, with good reason. The purpose of health care regulation is to protect patients from untrained or inadequate providers who would do them harm. . . . Restrictions of information and services do not take place in an open marketplace. The provider-patient relationship is inherently unequal, and the denial of information or services directly impacts the patient's health and well-being. Contemporary debates over refusals and denials of care have disproportionately focused on philosophical issues of balancing patients' rights and providers' beliefs. This framing fails to address the real life consequences refusals and denials of care have for patient health. . . .

Refusals and denials of care threaten the consistency of health care by allowing professionals to base their treatment decisions on religious and moral beliefs that fall outside the purview of professional discretion. As a result, patient access to care is constrained by the specific professional or institution from whom she seeks care. . . .

Delivering quality care requires that health care professionals provide information and care consistent with the highest standards of scientific evidence, based on individual patient need, and with the goal of maximizing wellness. . . . The failure of health care professionals to provide information regarding or access to specific types of health care is not solely an exercise of individual conscience but rather the provision of substandard care.

*Susan Berke Fogel and Tracy A. Weitz, "Health Care Refusals: Undermining Quality Care for Women," National Health Law Program, 2010. www.healthlaw.org.*

impose their religious beliefs on their employees, regardless of whether they share their employer's objection to contraceptive use. Indeed, the opposition to contraceptive use by some religious leaders and individuals does not reflect the beliefs or actions of the vast majority of Americans: Contraceptive use by women of all faiths—including Catholics and evangelicals and those who attend religious services most frequently—is the overwhelming norm in U.S. society.

Requiring for-profit companies to cover the full range of FDA-approved methods for the prevention of pregnancy without any out-of-pocket costs is sound public health policy and contributes to the social and financial well-being of women and their families. Thanks to the contraceptive coverage guarantee that went into effect starting in August 2012, millions of U.S. women are already able to obtain contraceptive services and supplies without cost-sharing. This major advance for women's health should not be taken away from any of those who already enjoy it—nor should it be denied to any women who stand to gain this benefit going forward.

"Freedom of conscience protections . . .
acknowledge that certain demands of
patients, usually for procedures that are
life-destructive and not life-saving,
must not be blindly accommodated to
the detriment of the rights of healthcare providers."

# Conscience Protection Laws Preserve Religious Freedom and Do Not Endanger Women's Health

*Denise M. Burke and Anna Franzonello*

*Denise M. Burke and Anna Franzonello are, respectively, vice president of legal affairs and staff counsel of Americans United for Life, a pro-life organization. In the following viewpoint, Burke and Franzonello detail how health care providers' right to refuse to participate in abortion procedures or other services that violate their religious beliefs is under attack by abortion advocates and their supporters. The authors contend that access to abortion services is not a right guaranteed by the Constitution or*

Denise M. Burke and Anna Franzonello, "A Primer on Protecting Healthcare Freedom of Conscience," Defending Life 2012. Americans United for Life, 2012, pp. 555-563.

*any law, nor is there any current law that provides total protection of conscience. Rather than a politically motivated movement of the conservative, far right-wing, the effort to protect conscience rights of health care providers is assumed to be part of the First Amendment of the US Constitution. The authors argue that conscience protection laws do not endanger patients, but threats to eliminate conscience protection laws do threaten patient care.*

As you read, consider the following questions:

1. Why was an Illinois ambulance driver fired, according to the authors?

2. What percentage of ACOG members stopped delivering babies in 2006, as reported by Burke and Franzonello?

3. Who is Michael Mennuti, as discussed by the authors?

Cathy Cenzon DeCarlo began her nursing career in her home country of the Philippines. In 2001, she moved to the United States, eager to continue to serve as a nurse and excited about the opportunity to work on interesting and challenging cases. A practicing Roman Catholic, Nurse DeCarlo's conscientious objection to participating in abortion procedures was known by her employer, The Mount Sinai Hospital, since her job interview in 2004. However, in May 2009, under the threat of disciplinary action—including possible termination and loss of her license—Nurse DeCarlo was forced to participate in a late-term abortion. Coerced participation in abortion was a nightmare, not a fulfillment of the "American dream," for Nurse DeCarlo.

Nurse DeCarlo's story is just one example of the concerted attack on the rights of conscience of America's healthcare providers—an attack that threatens not just conscience, but the entire stability of our healthcare system as a whole.

# A Concerted Attack on Conscience

Over the last few decades, abortion advocates and their allies have launched a concerted campaign to force hospitals, healthcare institutions, health insurers, and individual healthcare providers to provide, refer, or pay for abortions.

Their determined efforts to eviscerate the concept of conscience and the freedom to follow one's religious, moral, or ethical beliefs from the medical profession have resulted in the following:

- Catholic Charities in New York and California being forced by their state supreme courts to face the unenviable choice of offering healthcare coverage for contraceptives (even though the use of artificial contraception violates long-standing Catholic teachings) or, alternatively, to eliminate their prescription drug benefits for employees (in contravention of Catholic Church teachings concerning the provision of just wages and benefits);

- An ambulance driver in Illinois being fired for refusing to take a woman to an abortion clinic;

- In 2004, New Mexico refusing to approve a community-owned hospital lease because of the hospital's refusal to perform elective abortions;

- A private hospital in Texas being sued for disregarding parental objections and providing life-sustaining care to an infant born after 23 weeks of gestation; and

- The Washington Board of Pharmacy dictating that pharmacists must, regardless of conscience or other objections, fill all prescriptions, including those for contraceptives and "emergency contraceptives."

Even where state and federal laws protect conscience rights, coercion and discrimination against healthcare professionals with conscientious objections are all too commonplace. For example:

- A nurse at The Mount Sinai Hospital in New York, Cathy DeCarlo was forced to participate in a late term abortion despite her conscientious objection. A federal court dismissed her claim, saying Nurse DeCarlo cannot bring suit by herself for a violation of federal law. Instead, ruled the court, the U.S. Department of Health and Human Services (HHS) can (if they choose) pursue her case under regulations enacted by the George W. Bush Administration.

- Nine nurses at Nassau University Medical Center in Long Island, New York, were suspended for refusing to participate in an abortion. Only after the nurses' union intervened did the hospital drop its disciplinary charges and apologize to the nurses.

- Vanderbilt University required applicants to its nursing program to take an abortion pledge. After a complaint was filed with HHS for a violation of federal law, Vanderbilt changed its abortion pledge policy.

Sadly, this represents only a small sampling of the mounting attacks on the freedom of healthcare professionals to provide medical care without violating their religious, moral, or ethical beliefs.

## Pro-Life Pharmacists Targeted

In recent years, abortion advocates and their allies have prominently targeted pro-life pharmacists. Their goal is to require pharmacists to dispense contraceptives (including "emergency contraceptives"), forcing them to choose between their livelihood and their deeply held religious, moral, or ethical beliefs. Although the U.S. Constitution protects the free exercise of religion, allowing one to follow what his or her conscience morally directs, the abortion lobby is turning the debate into a referendum on alleged "refusals" to provide women access to controversial reproductive procedures.

These groups recognize that if they can establish legal precedent to coerce someone to violate their conscience regarding contraceptives, they can then easily extend that legal precedent to coerce pharmacists to dispense RU-486 (the so-called "abortion pill"), to coerce medical students to participate in abortion training, and to coerce doctors to participate in surgical abortion.

## The History of Conscience Rights

Often thought of as a contemporary problem, the right of conscience was referenced and considered by our Founding Fathers. For example, Thomas Jefferson wrote, "No provision in our Constitution ought to be dearer to man than that which protects the rights of conscience against the enterprises of the civil authority." Moreover, traditional western thought has understood individual conscience to be a guide for action and indispensable to appropriate action.

In the face of these attacks on a right imbedded in our nation's history, it is necessary for states to take action. To that end, AUL [Americans United for Life] has drafted the "Healthcare Freedom of Conscience Act" to assist legislators seeking to protect the historic right of conscience.

## Avoiding Added Stress

Protecting the freedom of conscience of healthcare providers and institutions is necessary to avoid added stress on an already overtaxed healthcare system. Experts project that current shortages of physicians, nurses, and other healthcare professionals will worsen, failing to meet future requirements.

Legal action and other pressure to compel healthcare providers to participate in procedures to which they conscientiously object threaten to make the already dangerous situation disastrous. By forcing healthcare professionals to choose between conscience and career, we will lose doctors, nurses, and other healthcare providers who are already in short supply, especially in rural parts of the country, and will bar competent young men and women from entering these vital professions.

Many women have already experienced firsthand the current provider shortage, having a hard time finding obstetricians to deliver their babies. In 2006, 14 percent of ACOG [American College of Obstetricians and Gynecologists] members reported they had stopped delivering babies. Further, the American Association of Medical Colleges (AAMC) projects an anticipated physician shortfall of 91,500 or more by 2020.

## The Nursing Shortage

As troubling as these predictions are, the nursing shortage is even worse. Some studies predict the shortage of registered nurses (RNs) in the U.S. will reach 260,000 by 2020. Health Resources and Services Administration (HRSA) officials have projected the nation's nursing shortage could grow to more than one million nurses by 2020, and analysts show that all 50 states will experience a shortage of nurses to varying degrees by the year 2015. . . .

According to a July 2007 report released by the American Hospital Association, U.S. hospitals need approximately 116,000 RNs to fill current vacant positions nationwide. Moreover, over half of the surveyed nurses reported that they intended to retire between 2011 and 2020. The Council on Physician and Nurse Supply has determined that 30,000 additional nurses must graduate annually to meet the nation's emerging healthcare needs, an expansion of 30 percent of the current number of annual nurse graduates. . . .

There is an important public health interest in ensuring the protection of conscience rights; forcing healthcare professionals to choose between their consciences and their careers will only heighten the current healthcare provider shortage. In a survey conducted in 2008, 91 percent of faith-based physicians agreed with the statement, "I would rather stop practicing medicine altogether than be forced to violate my conscience."

To slow—and not exacerbate—these shortages, there is a need for comprehensive conscience protections and proper enforcement of existing federal and state laws. Model legislation providing such comprehensive protection is contained in AUL's "Healthcare Freedom of Conscience Act," which has already been enacted in Mississippi, Idaho, and Louisiana, and provides protection for all healthcare providers and all procedures.

Protecting rights of conscience does not ban any procedure or prescription and does not mandate any particular belief or morality. Freedom of conscience simply provides American men and women the guarantees that this country was built upon: the right to be free from coercion. Protecting conscience helps ensure providers enter and remain in the healthcare profession, helping to meet the rising demand for quality health care. Failing to do so will compromise basic health care for the entire nation. . . .

## Access to Abortion Is Not a Right

*Myth*: It is unconstitutional for healthcare providers to refuse to provide abortion because women have a legal right to obtain an abortion.

*Fact*: First, there is no right of access to abortion. In fact, the abortion right first announced in *Roe v. Wade* and reaffirmed in *Planned Parenthood v. Casey* is the right of a woman to choose whether to terminate a pregnancy without interference from the government. Those cases cannot legitimately be read to give any patient, let alone the government, the authority to violate the fundamental freedom of conscience by forcing a healthcare provider to perform an abortion or any other controversial procedure.

Laws that protect the civil rights of healthcare providers do not forbid women from obtaining abortions. They merely protect healthcare providers from acting contrary to their consciences by providing them a right to refrain from participating in an abortion.

In fact, the U.S. Supreme Court has expressly recognized that (federal or state) governments are not required to facilitate abortions by funding them. In *Harris v. McRae*, the Court upheld a federal ban on the use of federal Medicaid funds to pay for elective abortions. In its reasoning, the Court noted that the abortion right created in *Roe* did not establish an entitlement to abortion. Rather, the Court said, *Roe* merely created limits on state action. Similarly, in *Webster v. Reproductive Health Services*, the Court upheld a state statute that prohibited state-run medical centers from providing elective abortions. Therefore, legislation protecting the rights of healthcare providers to refrain from participating in or facilitating abortion does not place an impermissible burden on a woman's right to abortion, because women do not have a right to force an individual or institution, including the government, to provide it.

## Conscience Protection Laws Are Needed

*Myth*: Additional right of conscience protection is unnecessary because my state already has a conscience law.

*Fact*: Only two states—Louisiana and Mississippi—protect the rights of conscience of all healthcare providers, institutions, and payers (e.g., health insurance companies) who object to participating in any healthcare service based on a religious, moral, or ethical objection. Although 45 other states and the federal government have adopted conscience laws, these laws are inadequate because they usually protect the right to object only to participating in abortion and do not offer any affirmative protections. Moreover, many of the current laws do not protect all healthcare providers. For example, pharmacists are often excluded from coverage in these statutes and, therefore, are lacking affirmative protection of their right to decline to provide abortion-inducing drugs or drugs that may used in an assisted suicide.

## Conscience Protection Is American

*Myth*: Conscience protection is a movement of the "religious right" and is designed to promote one religious viewpoint.

*Fact*: Conscience is at the heart of the American experience. Most Americans recognize the religious freedom found in the First Amendment of the United States Constitution. It reads:

> Congress shall make no law respecting an establishment of religion, or prohibiting the free exercise thereof; or abridging the freedom of speech, or of the press; or the right of the people peaceably to assemble, and to petition the government for a redress of grievances.

What Americans may not realize is that an early draft of the Amendment written by James Madison included the following:

> The Civil Rights of none shall be abridged on account of religious belief or worship, nor shall any national religion be established, nor shall the full and equal rights of conscience be in any manner, nor on any pretext infringed.

Though not included in the final version, it is fair to say that it was assumed by the Founders to be included therein.

Obviously, conscience protections did not spring up recently—say, during the Vietnam War era—but are a longstanding part of the nation's fabric. It is also a pluralistic right, one embraced by Christians and non-Christians alike. It is not based on respecting one faith but on respecting the integrity of all individuals.

## Affirming Quality Care

*Myth*: Legal protection for healthcare providers' freedom of conscience will endanger the lives of patients because it will allow healthcare providers to decline to provide healthcare services and thereby deny access to patients.

*Fact*: Freedom of conscience protections affirm the need to provide quality care to patients and do not interfere with existing medical malpractice standards. They merely acknowledge that certain demands of patients, usually for procedures that are life-destructive and not life-saving, must not be blindly accommodated to the detriment of the rights of healthcare providers.

Individuals and institutions do not lose their right to exercise their moral and religious beliefs and conscience once they decide to become healthcare providers. Nothing in the laws protecting healthcare freedom of conscience prevents others from providing the healthcare service to which a conscientious objection has been made. Conscientious objections are most often raised concerning elective services, such as abortion, contraception, sterilization, physician-assisted suicide, and withdrawal of nutrition and hydration, rather than necessary or lifesaving services. Therefore, the lack of participation in these practices by a healthcare provider or institution will not endanger the lives of patients.

## No Fundamental Right to Care

Further, abortion proponents are increasingly couching their arguments in the language of women's "rights to healthcare access." It is worth noting that there is no fundamental right to health care and, therefore, no overriding duty to provide it against one's conscience. Also, the term "access" is a red herring, as there is no real problem with a patient going to another healthcare provider for service.

Moreover, legal action and other pressure to compel healthcare providers to participate in procedures to which they conscientiously object threaten to exacerbate projected healthcare provider shortages. By forcing healthcare professionals to choose between conscience and career, we will lose doctors, nurses, and other healthcare professionals. It will also effectively bar competent young men and women, desperately needed, from entering these vital professions. Thus, "access" to health care is best protected by protecting conscience rights.

In addition, conscience is a check and balance in a healthcare provider's decision-making process. In the rapidly developing medical field, ethical challenges abound. We want our medical professionals to exercise ethical behavior (i.e., behavior in accord with their conscience).

## The Threat Is Real

*Myth*: Threats to conscience rights are theoretical and far-fetched.

*Fact*: While protecting conscience rights is commonsense, coercion and discrimination against healthcare professionals is all too commonplace. Efforts to expand legal coercion are well underway and they include mandatory referral of patients. For example, on August 30, 2005, Michael Mennuti, the President of American College of Obstetrics and Gynecology (ACOG), wrote to the U.S. Congress, stating the official position of ACOG: "Doctors who morally object to abortion should be required to refer patients to other physicians who will provide the appropriate care." Recent actions by ACOG and the American Board of Obstetrics and Gynecology (ABOG) to make board certification or recertification dependent on compliance with ACOG's position on referrals for abortion furthers this coercive effort.

Such efforts by ACOG and ABOG are only the first steps. After forcing complicity, the next step will be the coercion of active participation in abortion and other objectionable services and procedures by morally objecting providers. Opponents of conscience usually argue that only individuals can or

# Health Care Conscience Rights Act

To amend the Patient Protection and Affordable Care Act to protect rights of conscience with regard to requirements for coverage of specific items and services, to amend the Public Health Service Act to prohibit certain abortion-related discrimination in governmental activities, and for other purposes ... Congress finds the following:

(1) As Thomas Jefferson declared to New London Methodists in 1809, "[n]o provision in our Constitution ought to be dearer to man than that which protects the rights of conscience against the enterprises of the civil authority".

(2) Jefferson's conviction on respect for conscience is deeply embedded in the history and traditions of our Nation, and codified in numerous Federal laws approved by congressional majorities and Presidents of both parties. . . .

(3) Following enactment of the Patient Protection and Affordable Care Act, the Federal Government has sought to impose specific requirements that infringe on the rights of conscience of those who offer or purchase health coverage. . . .

(5) Nurses and other health care providers have increasingly been subjected to discrimination for abiding by their conscience rather than providing, paying for, or referring for abortion.

(6) Conscience rights protections for health care providers are an important part of civil rights protections in Federal law and are indispensable to the continued viability of the health care system in the United States.

*HealthCare Conscience Rights Act, H.R. 940,*
*113th Congress, March 4, 2013.*

should have (limited) freedom of conscience. This is short-sighted and purposely misunderstands the notion that the mission of an organization or institution (such as a hospital or a healthcare insurer) is informed by the individuals con-trolling that organization or institution.

The strategy being used by abortion advocates and others to compel conscience is both clever and chilling. If they can create legal precedent to compel violation of conscience for one procedure (e.g., dispensing contraceptives) or group of healthcare providers (e.g., pharmacists), they will have estab-lished the legal precedent necessary to compel doctors to par-ticipate in surgical abortion and to compel all healthcare pro-viders to participate in other objectionable procedures and services.

> "The Department of Health and Human Services is interpreting the new health care law in a manner that imposes health care directives and associated conscience concerns that extend well beyond the context of abortion."

# The Birth Control Coverage Mandate Violates Religious Freedom and Reduces Women's Access to Care

*Jeff Fortenberry*

*Jeff Fortenberry is a Republican congressman representing the First Congressional District of Nebraska. In the following viewpoint, Fortenberry testifies before the US House Energy and Commerce Committee's Subcommittee on Health regarding his opposition to mandated coverage for contraception and abortion services under the Affordable Care Act. Fortenberry asserts that the protection of the rights of conscience is a traditional American value, and that it is under threat by the mandate. He outlines his aim in drafting H.R. 1179, the Respect for Rights of Conscience Act of 2011 as an attempt to address that threat.*

Statement of Congressman Jeff Fortenberry: "Do New Health Law Mandates Threaten Conscience Rights and Access to Care?", House Energy and Commerce Subcommittee on Health, November 2, 2011.

*Fortenberry concludes that because faith-based providers of health care are being forced by the Affordable Care Act to deny services and coverage for the needy, the most vulnerable members of society will suffer.*

As you read, consider the following questions:

1. What percentage of Americans polled, according to Fortenberry, oppose forced funding of abortion-on-demand?

2. What does Fortenberry state as being the true intent of the Mikulski Amendment?

3. To what does the author attribute ballooning health care costs?

I am not a doctor, nor do I approach this hearing with clinical expertise or experience in the health care industry. I am speaking today as an American, as the representative of the First District of Nebraska, as a husband and father of five who is deeply concerned about the direction of our public policies, and in particular the direction of U.S. health care policy pursuant to the enactment of the health care overhaul last year [2010].

In 2009, I was pleased to hold several Town Hall events on health care, including one on August 27 at the People's City Mission in Lincoln, to discuss the many concerns my constituents sought to raise about access to quality health care. Over the past two years, there has been much debate about improving access to quality care as well as improving health care outcomes for hard-working Americans. I support the right type of health care reform that improves outcomes while reducing unsustainable costs. It grieves me profoundly that the health care law enacted in 2010 [the Affordable Care Act] represents the flash point of an ideological agenda that in no small measure threatens to undermine fundamental liberties that have defined the essence of our national character, particularly the foundational liberties of religion and conscience.

## The Right of Conscience

In 1809, Thomas Jefferson declared that "[n]o provision in our Constitution ought to be dearer to man than that which protects the rights of conscience against the enterprises of the civil authority." James Madison also spoke to the primacy of conscience in American public life when he stated in one of his amendments to the Constitution that "the civil rights of none shall be abridged on account of religious belief or worship, nor shall any national religion be established, nor shall the full and equal rights of conscience be in any manner, or on any pretext, infringed." Madison, the major architect of our Constitution, also declared "conscience is the most sacred of all property." The right of conscience is clearly a quintessential American tradition.

## Conscience Rights Are Threatened

Yet conscience rights have come under attack. Two years ago [in 2009], when significant alarms were being raised about the potential for the health care overhaul to serve as a vehicle for forced funding of abortion-on-demand, which 72% of Americans polled oppose, I began working on the Respect for Rights of Conscience Act. In anticipation of concerns (which have recently been confirmed in the series of administrative actions taken by the Department of Health and Human Services this year [mandating insurance coverage for contraceptives]) I introduced the measure on March 17, 2011 with my colleague Dan Boren.

H.R. 1179, the Respect for Rights of Conscience Act of 2011, sets forth findings that illustrate the fundamental nature of the health care liberties my colleagues and I are working to defend. It seeks to preclude the broad potential for violation of fundamental rights of conscience inherent in new powers granted to the federal bureaucracy through the terms of the 2010 health care law, as interpreted by the Department of Health and Human Services.

## The Government Crossed a Line

The federal government crossed a line with the enactment of the 2010 health care law by establishing a framework for imposing coverage requirements that infringe on the rights of health care providers broadly, including insurers, purchasers of insurance, plan sponsors, beneficiaries, and individual or institutional health care providers. Unless adequate conscience and associated non-discrimination protections are enacted, the 2010 health care law effectively bars health care stakeholders from retaining existing insurance arrangements consistent with their moral and ethical convictions.

I believe that it is vital for Americans to understand that the Department of Health and Human Services is interpreting the new health care law in a manner that imposes health care directives and associated conscience concerns that extend well beyond the context of abortion.

While the abortion funding concern remains preeminent, the potential fallout from the Administration's approach to health care reform encompasses a much broader array of conscience concerns related to drugs and procedures that have always been considered elective in nature, and offer no prospect of helping to mitigate chronic diseases such as cancer, heart disease, and stroke—that consume 75 cents of every public health care dollar spent in the United States.

## The Definition of Preventive Care

Specifically, on February 18, 2011, the [Barack] Obama Administration's Department of Health and Human Services rescinded key portions of a regulation issued in 2009 to protect the conscience rights of health care providers. Subsequently, in July 2011, the Institute of Medicine (IOM) issued a recommendation to the Department of Health and Human Services to mandate coverage of certain items and services considered by IOM to qualify under the category of preventive care.

On August 3, 2011, the Department of Health and Human Services issued guidelines flowing from the IOM recommendations that require mandatory coverage of drugs and procedures at no cost to the recipient and fully funded by third party enrollees, regardless of their willingness to pay for items and services many Americans object to in good conscience. It is also disturbing that that the process the Department followed in issuing this mandate short-circuited established rulemaking and comment procedures in a rush to expedite availability of drugs and procedures that are distinctly unrelated to America's health care challenges, over the vigorous objections of Members of Congress, the public, and a wide range of health care providers, including small businesses seeking to provide adequate health care benefits for their employees.

Ironically, the Department's interpretation of the Mikulski Amendment, from which it purports to derive justification for assuming unto itself vast and arbitrary powers which rightfully belong to Americans concerning their private health care decisions, reaches significantly beyond that amendment's stated intent to ensure "that women get the kind of preventive screenings and treatments they may need to prevent diseases particular to women such as breast cancer and cervical cancer."

I also find it peculiar that the Recommendations of the U.S. Preventive Services Task Force for 2010–2011, set forth in The Guide to Clinical Preventive Services, make no mention of the drugs and procedures covered in the HHS directive.

## A Too-Narrow Conscience Exception

Moreover, the Department's guidelines incorporate such a narrowly construed conscience exception for religious provid-

## The Birth Control Mandate May Harm Women

It might turn out that the government's efforts to advance women—by advancing the contraceptive project—harm women. . . . This is possible because there is a rational and empirically supported possibility that women's freedom—including freedom from unwanted pregnancies, addictions, violence, and depression—is better achieved when women and men practice the virtues and disciplines expressed in the Christian and other churches' conscientious objection to the Mandate. . . . There is a great deal of evidence, in fact, indicating that women in particular benefit physically, mentally, and otherwise, from practicing the personal and religious disciplines flowing from these teachings. Consequently, there are good reasons to believe that their health will flourish in situations wherein the free exercise of religion is strongly protected. . . .

All of this is in addition to the practical observation that women would lose a great deal of health care if religious health care institutions were forced to go out of business due to the Mandate.

*Helen Alvaré,* Villanova Law Review, *2013.*

ers as to ensure that the vast majority of faith-based health care providers in the United States, including faith-based plans and employers such as parochial schools and universities, will be forced to either violate their deeply-held beliefs, drop health care coverage, or cease providing health care services to the general public unless they serve or employ persons primarily of their own faith. Such a scenario is discriminatory and insulting. To clarify potential misconceptions about the application of conscience rights to institutional health care providers, it is understood that 'providers' in this context includes entities managed by individuals working together to uphold fundamental moral and ethical convictions in the exercise of their beneficent mission.

For the first time in the history of the U.S. health care system, which owes its success in large measure to the faith-based institutions that continue to serve as a compassionate backstop for the health care needs of our most vulnerable and underserved populations, ill-advised public policies threaten to result in the following adverse consequences: 1) ballooning health care costs, by virtue of the extensive scope of mandated coverage; 2) absent the enactment of adequate conscience protections, the forced violation of deeply held beliefs of health care providers, who will be required by the strong arm of government to choose between their convictions and livelihood; 3) resulting in reduced access to high quality care for vulnerable populations that have traditionally relied on charitable institutions for health care.

I find it is deeply troubling that this country, which derived its unique character and strength from inalienable rights, including freedom of conscience, whether exercised in a religious context or otherwise, is increasingly facing the steady erosion of the right of health care providers to exercise deeply held moral and ethical judgments. Americans deserve a health care system that respects their core values and fundamental liberties to negotiate private health care decisions and treatment options, as has always been the case prior to the passage of the new health care law.

> *"[The mandate] . . . is not directed at the exercise of religion [but] allows each person to follow the precepts of his or her religion within the confines of one's own home and body."*

# The Birth Control Coverage Mandate Does Not Violate Religious Freedom and Increases Women's Access to Care

*Nitzan Weizmann*

*Nitzan Weizmann is a law student and the executive board president of the Harvard Women's Law Association. In the following viewpoint Weizmann notes that decisions about women's access to contraception following the passage of the Affordable Care Act are being considered and made without regard for a woman's perspective or the medical conditions treated with oral contraceptives. She asserts that the entire premise of the religious objections to contraceptive coverage mandates is false, because contraception does not end life, unlike abortion. She also argues*

Nitzan Weizmann, "Women's Access to Contraception Does Not Violate Employers' Religious Freedom," Harvard Civil Rights-Civil Liberties Law Review, March 1, 2012. Copyright © 2012 by Harvard University Law School. All rights reserved. Reproduced by permission.

101

*that objections to this coverage are based on a desire to control women and demean them by forcing them to defend their use of oral contraceptives for "legitimate medical reasons." Further, Weizmann maintains, since the mandate applies to all employers, faith-based and otherwise, there is no basis for or right to an exemption from the law.*

As you read, consider the following questions:

1. How many of the House Oversight and Government Reform Committee's witnesses at the February 16, 2012, hearing on the issue of contraception were women, according to the author?

2. How much does Weizmann say most women without insurance pay for contraception per month?

3. What Supreme Court case does Weizmann cite as part of the court's Free Exercise jurisprudence?

There's been a lot of talk recently about contraception. Mostly it has been about the fact that under the [President Barack] Obama healthcare reform, religious employers are required to provide their employees with health insurance that will provide contraception directly to the employee at no cost. The conversation has revolved around religious freedom and government intervention with the freedom of conscience of the employers. When the House Oversight and Government Reform Committee held a hearing on the issue of contraception on February 16, [2012,] it heard from two panels of witnesses. Out of 10 witnesses in all, one holds a medical degree; all are clergy or work for religious educational institutions. Of these, two are women. So it would seem the best method to inform our elected officials about the proper availability of contraceptives to the public is to hear from middle-aged men who specialize in religion, not medicine. But this is not about men, middle-aged or otherwise. The availability of oral contraception is about women and their health. Let us put aside for a moment the fact that the hearing was so one-sided that House Democrats walked out in protest. Let us, instead, focus on the simple fact that decisions about women's health, decisions about whether and when we bear children, decisions that influence the entire trajectory of a woman's life, are made without consideration of the central elements in any of these: a woman's perspective and the medical implications that result from taking or not taking oral contraceptives.

## Contraception Is Not Abortion

Oral contraceptives, known as birth control pills, are basically small doses of hormones that, when taken on a daily basis, prevent a woman's body from releasing an egg into the fallopian tube, thus preventing a pregnancy from beginning. That means that when birth control pills work, which is over 99% of the time, conception never takes place. This is a small but crucial fact that differentiates the contraceptive debate from the abortion debate.

The most oft-repeated line of the "pro-life" movement is that abortion should be illegal because life begins at conception, and therefore abortion is homicide—it is the ending of an existing life. This argument may not be persuasive, and it may entirely ignore serious questions of a woman's control over her body and her right not to serve as an incubator, but at least it has a grain of something that society as a whole agrees on—killing is, generally, wrong. But the recent tempest surrounding the issue of access to oral contraceptives reveals that the "pro-life" movement is really an anti-choice movement. Once we understand that there is no life that needs protecting other than that of the woman who is using the pills, this is truly about preventing women from exercising control over their own bodies, even when those are the only bodies involved. What is behind this frenzy is ostensibly a religious conviction—God, according to the Judeo-Christian tradition, commanded us humans to go forth and multiply. So

## Contraceptives Are Also Medicine

Under the provisions in the Affordable Care Act, women will have access to the care and family planning services they need without worrying about the cost. Women using contraception reduce their risk of developing ovarian and endometrial cancers at about half the rate of the rest of the population.

Contraception is used to treat or prevent many health conditions that affect women, including ovarian cysts, endometriosis, pelvic inflammatory disease, uterine fibroid tumors, abnormal bleeding, pain associated with ovulation, and anemia. Women who used oral contraceptives are also less likely to develop rheumatoid arthritis, particularly in its more severe forms.

*Organizing for Action, 2013. www.barackobama.com.*

giving women the choice of having a sex life and not getting pregnant interferes with God's plan, and we can't have that.

## A Hypocritical Position

This is not only completely hypocritical—after all, condoms are readily available at your local drugstore and/or vending machine, and health insurance plans cover vasectomies—it is also blind to the full range of uses of oral contraceptives. Birth control pills are, after all, nothing more than hormones. And hormones do a lot more than regulate pregnancy. Women of all ages use oral contraceptives regardless of whether they are sexually active in order to help manage various conditions, including highly irregular menstrual cycles, controlling excess facial hair, acne, bone thinning, and breast and ovarian cysts, among others. To these girls and women, oral contraception is medication. Denying women access to contraception is not just a method of creating more unplanned pregnancies; it is a method of ensuring that women who depend on it for their health are repeatedly humiliated as they try to get access to their medication, having to get special exemptions from their health insurance providers or paying upwards of $50 a month for it.

Imagine a young coed walking into her neighborhood pharmacy to pick up oral contraceptives. She uses the medication not for purposes of birth control but as part of the treatment of a fairly common hormonal disorder which impacts her appearance, as well as the regularity of her menstrual cycle. Ironically enough, she takes the pill so that someday, when she is ready, she can conceive without excruciating difficulty. When she goes to pay for the prescription, she is told that her insurer does not cover the medication—she can pay out of pocket and take the pills home, or she can call her insurance company and try to get them to cover the prescription because she uses it not for contraception but for "legitimate medical reasons." She spends the next few days on the phone with the health insurance company, running back and forth to the doctor, trying to gather the proof required to bring the contraceptive under her plan coverage. Eventually, she gives up and pays the full cost of the pills out of pocket. To avoid further humiliation, she stops trying to get the insurer to cover her medication and pays the full price every month. Before recent reforms to the healthcare market, this was not uncommon.

## Religion Is Not a Valid Exemption

Let us assume, however, that religion really is the impetus for all of this. Let us assume that what an employee does with her own body with oral contraceptives that she receives directly from the health insurance company, a workaround that was created precisely to protect the religious freedom of employers, somehow concerns the free exercise of the employers' religion. Under the current standard for free exercise cases, that doesn't really matter. Under the Supreme Court's current Free Exercise jurisprudence, most definitively laid out in *Employment Division v. Smith* (1990), religiously-motivated claims do not merit special exemptions from a facially neutral [does not explicitly discriminate against any person, entity, or belief system] law with a valid, non-discriminatory purpose. In this case, we are faced with neither facial discrimination nor an invidious [discriminatory, unfair, calculated to be hateful] purpose. The regulation applies to all employers, without exception, and it is not directed at the exercise of religion. This regulation allows each person to follow the precepts of his or her religion within the confines of one's home and body—and protects those of us who choose to follow different precepts than those of religious Conservatives.

Denying women the same access to oral contraceptives as they have to any other prescription medication is denying women access to an integral health care service. Reproductive freedom is women's health, and women's health concerns us all.

> "*Unlike contraception, the decision of whether or not to eat pork due to religious edicts does not involve major public health implications.*"

# The Public Good Is More Important than Religious Objections to Birth Control Coverage

*Jodi Jacobson*

*Jodi Jacobson is editor in chief of the website RH Reality Check. In the following viewpoint, she expresses outrage that the hearing to discuss the birth control mandate of the Affordable Care Act included no real evidence to support the denial of contraceptive coverage and that those testifying were almost exclusively men and all opposed contraception. The testimony, Jacobson argues, demonstrated that not only are the leaders of the religious antichoice front out of touch with women's health issues, they are dismissive of the rights of women in general. Not only do oral contraceptives help women and their families by allowing them to plan pregnancies, Jacobson contends, they help women for whom pregnancy would be life-threatening to avoid becom-*

*ing pregnant, as well as to relieve the symptoms of women afflicted with painful conditions. And, she argues, because contraception is so expensive, a law that provides greater access to it is needed and would save money for both insurance companies and tax payers by keeping women and families healthier.*

As you read, consider the following questions:

1. What did Congressman Darrell Issa say to chide his Democratic Party counterparts, according to Jacobson?

2. What percentage of sexually active Catholic women have used contraception, as reported by the author?

3. How many states require insurance plans to include coverage for contraception, according to Jacobson?

In his testimony at the February 16th, 2012 House Committee on Oversight and Government Reform hearing on the contraceptive coverage mandate under health reform, the Most Reverend William E. Lori, the Bishop of Bridgeport [Connecticut] and spokesman for the United States Conference of Catholic Bishops (USCCB), defended the claim of "religious freedom" by comparing the provision of essential primary health care for women to a kosher deli being forced to serve pork.

I'll call it the "ham sandwich defense."

This was but one of a series of you-had-to-be-there-to-believe-it episodes during a hearing on women's health care that featured nine male members of the religious right and only two female witnesses, all of whom in any case are opponents of the birth control mandate, and the majority of whom oppose the use of contraception per se; saw the constant and intentionally misleading re-definition by the religious right of modern methods of contraception as "abortifacients"; shut out not only the many religious leaders who support both the mandate and women's moral agency, but also medical and health professionals and witnesses who'd experienced denial of contraceptive care; and also featured constant and strident chiding by the Committee Chair, Congressman Darrell Issa (R-CA), of his Democratic Party counterparts that the hearing was "not about women's health, contraception, or health reform," while allowing all the anti-contraception, anti-health reform witnesses to speak about nothing but denying women health care, contraception, and health reform. The Democratic women representatives walked out of the hearing in protest.

## No Evidence

Moreover, not a single witness provided a compelling case for granting "conscience rights" to institutions, for why providing women insurance coverage for birth control would violate religious freedom, nor for why the accommodation created by the [Barack] Obama Administration to make sure women working in religiously-affiliated organizations that object to contraception can still get coverage of birth control without a co-pay created a burden for said institutions. In fact, not a single one provided any compelling reason whatsoever that any one's "conscience rights" trump access to a proven health intervention.

Which brings us back to pork.

## The Parable of the Kosher Deli

To illustrate the basic premise of his argument, Bishop Lori told what he called "The Parable of the Kosher Deli." In summary, Bishop Lori's parable told of a new law requiring that "any business that serves food must serve pork."

He continued:

There is a narrow exception for kosher catering halls attached to synagogues, since they serve mostly members of that synagogue, but kosher delicatessens are still subject to the mandate. The Orthodox Jewish community—whose members run kosher delis and many other restaurants and grocers besides—expresses its outrage at the new government mandate. And they are joined by others who have no problem eating pork—not just the many Jews who eat pork, but people of all faiths—because these others recognize the threat to the principle of religious liberty. They recognize as well the practical impact of the damage to that principle. They know that, if the mandate stands, they might be the next ones forced—under threat of severe government sanction—to violate their most deeply held beliefs, especially their unpopular beliefs. . . .

Bottom line: as the leading witness for the religious right, Bishop Lori made an astonishingly weak case by urging the nation to compare a fictitious law to override religious traditions governing whether or not to eat a certain type of meat with an actual law intended to dramatically expand access to contraception, a necessary, and often life-saving, essential public health intervention that the Bishops and other religious right denominations desperately do not want women to have.

## Contraception Benefits Women

While Congress is often swimming in "pork" [a term connoting politicians' directing of government funding to their own districts] (and there are many members these days who are, to put it mildly, full of baloney when it comes to facts) there is no foreseeable reason any government body in the United States would mandate that kosher delis must serve pork. There are, however, rational and compelling public health, medical, social, and economic justifications for providing universal health insurance coverage without a co-pay for birth control.

Modern contraception is recognized by the Centers for Disease Control, the World Health Organization, and virtually every major medical association as one of the ten greatest public health achievements of the 20th century. It enables women and men to voluntarily plan, space, and limit pregnancies and determine the ultimate size of their families. By reducing unintended pregnancies access to contraception also reduces the need for abortion. In fact, the use of contraception as a voluntary, responsible, and effective means of planning families is, as we have noted here repeatedly, virtually universal in the United States, where 99 percent of all sexually-active women and 98 percent of sexually-active Catholic women have used contraception.

Access to contraception also enables vulnerable women to avoid potentially life-threatening pregnancies (i.e. a woman with a serious heart condition or cancer might be advised to avoid pregnancy). It has been proven to dramatically reduce maternal death and disability, and *increase* infant and child survival. And it is a critical intervention for often painful, sometimes crippling conditions such as dysmenorrhea and polycystic ovary syndrome, which can affect young girls as early as age 11, and which the Department of Health and Human Services (HHS) estimates affects as many as 5 million women of childbearing age in the United States.

## Contraception Is Not Easily Accessed

Contrary to the recent protestations of many a male member of the United States Congress and many a male presidential candidate, contraception is not "available everywhere" nor is it "cheap." Paying for birth control pills can run a woman well over $600 per year, not including visits to the doctor for primary care and to obtain a prescription. Insertion of an IUD [intrauterine device] may carry a high initial cost of well over $1000.00. For students and low-income women, cost is the single most important factor impeding consistent access to birth control.

Providing birth control without a co-pay, however, yields enormous savings both for insurance companies and the public, something one could fairly assume to be attractive to those many bloviators [windbags] talking about government spending. And yet—no.

## Contempt for Women's Needs

By comparing coverage for a major public health intervention to a law mandating that kosher delis serve pork, Bishop Lori revealed just how out of touch the USCCB and the religio-patriarchy writ large are with the needs and rights of women to live as normal human beings, and profoundly trivialized the experiences of women who struggle to manage their fertility, their health, and the well-being of themselves and their families.

If nothing else, the ham sandwich defense underscored just how shallow legally, philosophically and practically is the "religious freedom" argument against access to contraception. It revealed just how desperate male patriarchal religious bodies and their political surrogates are to curtail the ability of women to make decisions about their bodies and their lives. And it laid bare once again the sheer digust and contempt many of them hold for actual, living, breathing women.

## No Legal Basis

Legally, the claim of "religious freedom" to deny women health care doesn't have a leg to stand on. As the American Civil Liberties Union (ACLU) has noted:

> [N]othing in the rule prevents anyone from espousing their beliefs about birth control or attempting to persuade others not to use it. The high courts of California and New York have rejected claims that requiring coverage of contraception somehow violates the First Amendment, and our courts have long held that institutions that operate in the public sphere are not above the law.

Moreover, as has been noted frequently at this point, 28 states already require insurance plans to include contraception, several with the same house-of-worship exception adopted by the administration and several with no exception at all. In several states, Catholic universities and other institutions already comply with state law in providing coverage for contraceptive care. In those that do not, women are often denied access to contraception even when their health and potentially their lives are at risk. How it can be viewed as moral or righteous to deny women basic health care is beyond me.

To my knowledge, unlike contraception, the decision of whether or not to eat pork due to religious edicts does not involve major public health implications. Somehow the sheer banality of this parable escaped whomever it was that drafted Bishop Lori's testimony.

Contraception is not a side of bacon in a kosher deli, but maybe if it were pork in a barrel we'd get universal access.

# Periodical and Internet Sources Bibliography

*The following articles have been selected to supplement the diverse views presented in this chapter.*

| | |
|---|---|
| Katie J. M. Baker | "Conservatives Think Your 'Conscience' Deserves More Rights than Your Uterus," *Jezebel*, March 5, 2013. http://jezebel.com. |
| Joan Frawley Desmond | "Proposed Health Care Conscience Rights Act—'Last and Only Hope'?," *National Catholic Register*, March 5, 2013. |
| Jacob Glass | "Religion and Reproductive Rights: Looking for Common Ground," NewSecurityBeat, September 23, 2013. www.newsecuritybeat.com. |
| Karen Gullo | "Obamacare Birth Control Mandate Ruled Unconstitutional," Bloomberg, November 2, 2013. www.bloomberg.com. |
| Frank G. Kirkpatrick | "The Role of Religious Ethics in Public Policy," *Huffington Post*, August 9, 2013. www.huffingtonpost.com. |
| Napp Nazworth | "Religious Freedom Concerns Continue After Mandate Revision," ChristianPost, February 6, 2013. www.christianpost.com. |
| Pew Research Religion and Public Life Project | "The Contraception Mandate and Religious Liberty," February 1, 2013. www.pewforum.org. |
| William L. Saunders | "Let Your Conscience Be Your Guide," Family Research Council, April 15, 2013. www.frc.org. |
| Sally Steenland | "Contraception Mandate Strengthens Religious Liberty and Women's Health," *Huffington Post*, March 20, 2013. www.huffingtonpost.com |

OPPOSING
VIEWPOINTS®
SERIES

CHAPTER 3

# What Clinical Concerns Impact Women's Health?

# Chapter Preface

Gender-specific medicine is an approach to health care wherein practitioners, knowing that men's and women's bodies respond differently to illness, medication, and the aging process, tailor their treatment plans according to the patient's sex. In the case of women's health in particular, this approach brings a fresh perspective, because women for decades were not included in medication trials or health studies, and so their unique responses to medications and different symptoms of illnesses were not recorded, let alone factored into treatment plans. In a 2012 paper published in *Academic Emergency Medicine*, physicians Alyson J. McGregor and Esther Choo provide the example of the drug digoxin, which has been used, they note, "to treat heart failure for more than 200 years," but which during the last decade has been shown to increase the risk of death among women with heart failure and depressed left ventricular systolic function: "Failure to conduct sex-specific analyses in the original trial of digoxin in congestive heart failure initially missed the significant harm of this treatment to women."

In a March 2011 article in *Haaretz*, a major Jewish newspaper, Esti Ahronovitz, relating an example provided by psychologist Maya Lavie-Ajayi, states that "a famous major study in 1988 . . . found that one aspirin a day was beneficial. The study looked at 22,000 men, and not a single woman. Today it is known that aspirin has a different effect on men, in whom it helps prevent heart attacks, and on women, in whom it has little effect on the heart, but may help prevent strokes."

Health research is only one area of medicine that stands to benefit from paying attention to the differences in the sexes. Emergency medicine providers stand to greatly enhance their ability to diagnose and treat heart attacks in women. Studies have shown that not only is postmenopausal women's vulnerability to heart attack nearly as great as men's but that women's heart attack symptoms are often very different from men's. Ahronovitz quotes gender-specific medicine expert Marek Glezerman, who explains,

> The classic picture of a heart attack . . . is a man clutching his left side and doubling over in intense pain that radiates to the shoulder and arm. But for one out of five women, the symptoms of a heart attack are totally different: the attack develops very gradually and not all at once. The woman complains of shortness of breath, the pain can radiate to the back of the neck, to the back or the jaw. And by the time she gets to the emergency room, the risk that she will be sent home with a diagnosis of hysteria is four times greater than for a man. And even when she obtains a diagnosis, the processes that surround it, the referral to a cardiologist or for catheterization, will take a lot longer than for a man.

But while some experts embrace gender-specific medicine as a beneficial system of providing optimal care to both men and women, other commentators are less optimistic. Sarah H. Moore begins her 2010 essay in *Body & Society*, which examines gender-specific medicine through the lens of feminist thought, with a quote by Barbara Ehrenreich and Deirdre English, from their 1977 book *Complaints and Disorders: The Sexual Politics of Sickness*: "Medicine's prime contribution to sexist ideology has been to describe women as sick." Moore cautions against what she describes as a gendered ideal of health that views traditional feminine traits as "healthy"; such a view is, she argues, as damaging as any sexist or misogynist view. Rather than leading to a greater valuation of women, the emphasis on feminine traits in a gender-specific medical approach leads to a view of the body as something that must be controlled, as a representation of the person as a whole, and as a symbol of goodness. This emphasis is dangerous for women and for men, Moore argues, because they lose sight of their larger selves and become hyperfocused on controlling their bodies rather than expanding their minds.

Gender-specific medicine is one women's health issue that concerns health care professionals and patients alike. Two other clinical concerns discussed by authors of the viewpoints in the following chapter are whether to make birth control pills available for over-the-counter purchase without a prescription and whether the 2009 US Preventive Services Task Force recommendations for mammography screening are appropriate and better for women's health outcomes.

"*The potential harms related to* failing *to detect breast cancer as early as possible . . . [are] sure to be a consequence from recommending against routine screening mammography.*"

# US Preventive Services Task Force Mammography Guidelines Put More Women at Risk

*Elisa Rush Port*

*Elisa Rush Port is chief of breast surgery at Mt. Sinai School of Medicine in New York City and codirector of the Dubin Breast Center. In the following viewpoint, Port rejects the US Preventive Task Force's recommendation for women under the age of fifty to forgo annual mammograms. According to Port, the task force's decision was arbitrary and not grounded in an accurate interpretation of the available data. The survival benefit from annual mammography for all women forty and over is the same. And, Port contends, there are measures other than survival that should be considered in evaluating the efficacy of mammography, such as reducing harm, anxiety, and costs. Other screening tests, like*

*CT scans and colonoscopy, the author maintains, continue to be broadly recommended despite their risks and limitations, and there should not be a different standard applied to mammography. Port adds that the risk of anxiety and stress is greater for women who do not have the benefit of early detection or the reassurance of annual screening.*

As you read, consider the following questions:

1. According to Port, in what year were the recommendations for yearly mammograms for women beginning at age forty established?

2. How many mammograms needed to be done in women aged thirty-nine to forty-nine before one cancer was detected, as reported by the author?

3. What are the risks associated with colonoscopy, according to Port?

There have been six major clinical trials and multiple others evaluating the efficacy of mammography and its role in the early detection of breast cancer. Cumulatively, these trials have demonstrated a clear-cut survival benefit across *all* age groups beginning at 40 years old. As a result, in 2002 recommendations were established for yearly screening mammography for women beginning at age 40 in the United States

In 2009, this recommendation was questioned when the United States Prevention Services Task Force (USPSTF) revisited the issue and published its findings in the *Annals of Internal Medicine*. Although the same data was analyzed and the survival benefit across all age groups (beginning at age 40) was demonstrated to be 15 percent or greater, the USPSTF's recommendations changed substantially. Instead of a "B" recommendation ("The USPSTF recommends the service. There is high certainty that the net benefit is moderate or there is moderate certainty that the net benefit is moderate to substantial"), screening mammography was downgraded to a

"D" ("The USPSTF recommends against the service. There is moderate or high certainty that the service has no net benefit or that the harms outweigh the benefits")

So what happened?

Essentially, there was a shift in thinking toward the "harms" and "costs" of mammography: unnecessary callbacks and biopsies, anxiety, and dollars. According to the USPSTF, the harms of yearly mammography outweighed the benefits for most age groups. According to the study published in the *Annals of Internal Medicine* that was everywhere in the press in 2009, the main reason for demoting mammography for women under the age of 50 was that for women 39 to 49, 1,904 mammograms were needed to be done to detect one cancer, compared with 1,339 mammograms for women 50 to 59. An arbitrary line was drawn in the sand by the USPSTF: 1 cancer detected in 1,339 mammograms was acceptable, but 1 cancer in 1,904 was not.

Thus the recommendation for yearly mammography in patients from 40 to 49 was rescinded. The study recommended forgoing mammography for this younger age group despite acknowledging that the survival benefit for the younger group was *the same.*

On top of that, a recent editorial in *The British Medical Journal* (*BMJ*) criticizing the Komen Foundation for its promotion of mammography suggested that Komen was overselling the benefits of mammography while saying nothing of the potential harms that screening mammography can engender.

## No Screening Test Is Perfect

There is no perfect screening test. Chest computerized tomography (known as CT scans) for lung cancer, for example, can lead to multiple follow-up exams that involve significant amounts of radiation. And if something suspicious is found on a chest CT, biopsy may be recommended, which could lead to major interventions such as lung surgery or complications

## Annual Mammograms Are Necessary for Finding Breast Cancer Early

The American Cancer Society is not changing our recommendations for breast cancer screening as a result of this report. Based on our initial review of this new guideline, we see no reason to change a strategy that has proven effective in reducing the death rates for breast cancer in all age groups, including those women ages 40–49....

Until we have something better, what we have to work with to detect breast cancer early is the screening mammogram. Is it imperfect? Yes. Has it saved lives and reduced deaths from breast cancer? Absolutely.

And that is the fact that simply cannot be ignored.

*J. Leonard Lichtenfeld, Dr. Len's Cancer Blog,*
*November 16, 2009. www.cancer.org.*

such as collapse of the lung. Colonoscopy, too—widely accepted as a life-saving screening test—can lead to bleeding, infection, and perforation, all of which are potentially life-threatening. There is no accurate screening test for ovarian cancer, which is why the majority of ovarian cancers are detected in Stage III or IV. We are dissatisfied when there is no good screening test, yet there are those who severely criticize the use of the effective ones that we have. What gives?

Mammography has withstood the tests of time, randomized clinical trials, and the introduction of other competing technologies, none of which have proven to be as effective for screening for breast cancer in the general population. The potential "harms" of mammography (follow-up exams, biopsies, and anxiety) that are constantly harped on by its critics are nowhere near as dangerous as those associated with other screening tests, and none of the potential harms is even close to being life-threatening. There is no question that with health care costs exploding, any test that results in downstreaming costs (which is basically *all* tests) must be scrutinized for the overall benefits.

But we have been there and done that with mammography. Neither the *Annals of Internal Medicine* study nor the recent editorial in *BMJ* factored into the discussion, in a full-fledged way, the potential harms related to *failing* to detect breast cancer as early as possible—which is sure to be a consequence from recommending against routine screening mammography. The *BMJ* editorial harshly criticized the Komen advertisement, implying that it numerically misrepresented the survival benefit of screening mammography. But here are the facts: There *is* a survival benefit, across all age groups, among those who develop breast cancer and have been screened with mammography. And while survival has always been the gold standard for evaluating the efficacy of a screening test, there are other, almost equally as important, endpoints that demonstrate significant benefits of mammography, including reduction in harm, anxiety, and cost.

For example, the development and widespread use of mammography in the 1970s and 1980s was the single most influential factor leading to the development of breast-conserving surgery, or lumpectomy: a smaller procedure with no overnight hospital stay, and with an equal survival rate, that allows patients to return to work, family, and activity much more quickly than a mastectomy. In the United States in 2012, the majority of women who are eligible for lumpectomy surgery choose this option.

## Forgoing Testing Causes Stress

Critics talk about the anxiety and stress related to getting mammograms. What about the anxiety and stress related to *not* getting mammograms? For the woman who isn't getting yearly mammograms, isn't it stressful to know that if one day she feels a lump, and that lump is found to be cancer, it is likely to be larger and require more extensive surgery and chemotherapy than if she had been screened?

While anecdotes and personal experience are not criteria for making recommendations for the general population, those of us who take care of breast cancer patients on a daily basis and make it our life's work see cases every day exemplifying why mammography works. Yes, there are cancers that are missed on mammogram. And yes, there are patients who do *not* get mammograms who develop breast cancers that are completely curable and survivable. But for the vast majority of women, the data clearly shows that mammograms save lives and result in less invasive and extensive treatment for many women. The harms related to mammography are exaggerated and need to be kept in perspective as mostly tolerable and completely non-life-threatening. When it comes to recommending yearly mammograms and affirming that mammograms save lives, let's stop getting hung up on technicalities. Let's stop re-crunching the numbers until they give us a different answer, and accept what the data demonstrates: From age 40—not age 50—yearly mammograms save lives.

*"Overall, there was no clear change in [breast cancer] screening rates after the USPTF's recommendation."*

# New Guidelines Did Not Change Mammography Rates

*Genevra Pittman*

*Genevra Pittman is a medical journalist for Reuters Health. In the following viewpoint, Pittman reports that despite the 2009 recommendation by the US Preventive Services Task Force (USPSTF) that women under fifty should not have annual mammograms to screen for breast cancer, the rate of screening did not decline among women in any age group. Professional organizations such as the American College of Obstetricians and Gynecologists (ACOG) still recommend annual screening beginning at age forty and cite some experts who believe that it will take some time, but there will be a decline in screening rates eventually. Pittman indicates that researchers recommend that women be fully aware of the risks and benefits associated with screening and make an informed decision.*

As you read, consider the following questions:

1. What, according to Pittman, does Dr. Michael LeFevre say is the probable reason that mammography rates did not change?

2. As reported by the author, what percentage of women said in 2011 that they had recently had a mammogram?

3. According to Pittman, what does David Howard suppose providers do when there are conflicting versions of guidelines?

The proportion of women undergoing screening for breast cancer every year did not change after a government-backed panel said women in their 40s shouldn't have routine mammograms, according to a new study.

In 2009, the U.S. Preventive Services Task Force (USPSTF) recommended that women aged 50 to 74 have a mammogram every other year and said for younger women, screening should be an individual decision by each woman with her doctor.

That's because the benefits of screening only slightly outweigh harms from overdiagnosis and unnecessary treatment, and any potential benefits are smaller in younger women, according to Dr. Michael LeFevre, co–vice chair of the Task Force.

LeFevre, who is also a family medicine doctor at the University of Missouri School of Medicine in Columbia, said he didn't find the new results all that surprising.

"It would be optimistic to think the lack of change reflects the decision by many women in their 40s to go ahead and proceed with mammography with a clear understanding of the benefits as well as the risks," he told Reuters Health.

"I think it is a bit more likely that physicians continue to recommend mammography without necessarily discussing the

## Mammography Rates Have Remained Stable

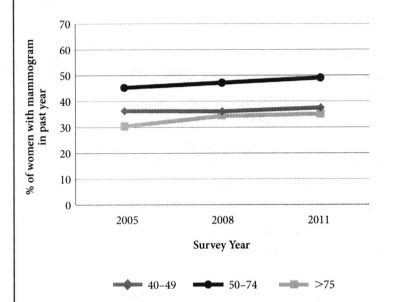

### Adjusted rates of mammography in the past year

| Age group | 2005 Weighted % | 2008 Weighted % | 2011 Weighted % | p-value for 2011 vs. 2008* |
|---|---|---|---|---|
| All ages | 50.5 | 51.9 | 53.6 | 0.07 |
| 40–49 | 46.3 | 46.1 | 47.5 | 0.38 |
| 50–74 | 55.3 | 57.2 | 59.1 | 0.09 |
| >75 | 40.4 | 44.3 | 45.1 | 0.84 |

*P-values based on logistic regression camparing the change in mammography rates from 2008 to 2011, adjusted for all variables in Table 1.

TAKEN FROM: Lydia E. Pace, Yulei He, and Nancy L. Keating, "Trends in Mammography Screening Rates After Publication of the 2009 US Preventive Services Task Force Recommendations," *Cancer*, vol. 119, no. 14, July 2013.

specifics of what the science tells us," said LeFevre, who wasn't involved in the new study. "It's always easier to do than to discuss."

Dr. Lydia Pace from Brigham and Women's Hospital in Boston and her colleagues analyzed nationally-representative surveys of close to 28,000 women, age 40 and older, from 2005, 2008 and 2011. Among other things, women were asked if they'd had a mammogram in the past year.

Overall, there was no clear change in screening rates after the USPSTF's recommendation: 53.6 percent of all women said they'd recently had a mammogram in 2011, compared to 51.9 percent in 2008.

Mammography rates did not change in any age group. Among women in their 40s, 47.5 percent had been recently screened as of 2011, compared to 46.1 percent in 2008.

Some professional organizations, such as The American College of Obstetricians and Gynecologists, still recommend regular screening for women as young as 40—and surveys suggest many doctors favor that approach.

"When there are conflicting versions of guidelines, providers may err on the side of screening," said David Howard, a health policy researcher from Emory University in Atlanta who has studied mammography.

One of the issues is that both individual women and guideline-making groups may weigh the benefits and harms of mammography differently, researchers said.

Some may accept any risk for a small chance of catching breast cancer early, whereas others will weigh the harms of infection and bleeding from biopsies, for example, more heavily.

Howard said that over time, there may be a shift toward fewer women in their 40s having mammograms.

Because the guidelines are relatively recent, "A lot of women in that age group turned 40 with the expectation that they would get a mammogram every year or every other year," Howard, who also wasn't part of the new research team, told Reuters Health.

"I think it's a harder thing to stop screening if you've already started," Pace agreed. "That could account for some of the lack of decline."

However, she told Reuters Health, "Given how widespread the publicity was about these recommendations, I think most providers were certainly aware of them, and we would have expected to see some changes we didn't see."

Researchers said women in their 40s should be fully informed about the benefits and risks of screening before deciding to have a mammogram.

"For younger women," Pace said, "the decision to undertake mammography screening is one that is not necessarily taken lightly."

"Be aware that there is some benefit—the benefit is quite small, there are some risks and that a personal decision is absolutely to be honored," LeFevre said.

> *"Though making birth control accessible over the counter would ... make it more affordable for those that cannot currently afford contraceptives, the health risks outweigh the cost benefits."*

# Over-the-Counter Birth Control Would Pose Risks

*Morgan Greenwald*

*Morgan Greenwald is a student at the University of Southern California, majoring in neuroscience and health promotion and disease prevention studies. In the following viewpoint, Greenwald argues that birth control pills should only be available by prescription. A doctor's supervision is vital, she contends, to ensure that women are screened for potentially dangerous health conditions prior to starting the pill and to ensure that they are monitored for other side effects, such as depression, while taking the pill. Women are not able to discern whether they are experiencing side effects, and since those side effects can be dangerous, a doctor's supervision is needed, the author maintains. Greenwald concludes that since over-the-counter availability would only lower the cost of birth control pills and increase access to*

*them for a small percentage of women, it is not worth the poten-*
*tial risks to the majority of women that would come with such*
*availability.*

As you read, consider the following questions:

1. What are the consequences of taking rifampin and birth control pills at the same time, according to Greenwald?

2. What is one of the main side effects of birth control pills, according to the author?

3. What percentage of Americans were uninsured in 2010, according to Greenwald?

Last week the American College of Obstetricians and Gynecologists released new recommendations stating its support for over-the-counter oral contraceptives. Currently, birth control is only accessible per a doctor's prescription. By making the drug available over the counter, patients would have definite benefits—potentially lowering the price of birth control, increasing access for women and saving health insurance companies money—but at what cost?

The biggest danger that would come with birth control becoming an over-the-counter drug is the loss of a very crucial role that doctors play in prescriptions. If it's available over the counter, women will no longer be required to see a doctor before beginning the pill: They will not be screened by a doctor for risks prior to use of birth control, they will not be able to determine whether they are experiencing detrimental side effects after going on the pill and they will have no way of deciding which type of birth control is suited for them in conjunction with other prescription medications they might be taking or other health issues. Because of this, birth control should remain a drug that is solely prescribed by doctors after consultation.

There are numerous examples of the negative health impacts of over-the-counter availability. One is birth control's

## Many Physicians Oppose Over-the-Counter Oral Contraceptives

Of the 638 obstetricians, gynecologists and family practitioners interviewed in "Physician Attitudes Toward Over the Counter Availability for Oral Contraceptives," a large majority—71 percent—said they were against over-the-counter hormonal contraceptives. More than 90 percent of respondents cited safety as their primary concern.

*Christine M. Williams,*
*Catholic News Service, January 11, 2013.*

interaction with a common antibiotic, rifampin. If a woman is taking rifampin and birth control at the same time, the contraceptive loses its ability to prevent pregnancies, and it is recommended by doctors to use a second type of birth control when prescribed rifampin. According to *Women's Health Magazine*, birth control also puts women slightly more at risk for blood clots, especially those who already exhibit cardiovascular risk factors, such as high blood pressure or diabetes, or those who smoke.

A proponent might suggest including extra warning labels, which raises another issue: If birth control becomes an over-the-counter drug, are the drug's warning labels enough of a precaution if the side effects are too serious?

The warnings that accompany any given birth control are endless, and as such over-the-counter birth control would require multiple warning labels that most women would not likely read. Even a warning provided in a supplemental small booklet might not be sufficient enough to warn someone that birth control will not be effective for them. There is no replacement for a doctor explaining to a woman in person not only the general known side effects of a drug, but how it will affect her specifically.

But one of the main side effects of birth control, mood swings, is one that can affect any person regardless of health conditions or habits, and a warning label would not suffice to address this.

In a 2008 Health.com article on common birth control side effects, Dr. Hilda Hutcherson, an ob-gyn [obstetrics and gynecology] professor at Columbia University explained the complexities of dealing with this.

"If it's really the birth control and not some other factor that's bringing you down, you may need to find a nonhormonal method," she said.

How would a woman know that her depression is a result of her birth control without consulting a doctor, and then know what different kind of birth control to change to? A drug with a possible side effect as serious as depression renders a consultation with a doctor necessary.

Another pro-over-the-counter argument relates to money. The monetary advantages of making birth control more accessible are minimal, to such an extent that they do not justify the health risks. Under Obama's Affordable Care Act, birth control is covered by insurance as a prescription medicine only. In 2010, 16.3 percent of Americans were uninsured according to CNN, meaning drug companies would be making a decision that would be cost beneficial to every one in nine people.

Though making birth control accessible over the counter would relinquish doctor fees and make it more affordable for those that cannot currently afford contraceptives, the health risks outweigh the cost benefits.

As *Iowa State Daily* reporter Leah Hansen wrote Monday, "It would be up to the women to know which brand and dose she needs, what are the side effects, what other medications may interfere with birth control and any other questions she might have regarding the product."

Doctors are part of the birth control process for a reason: to warn patients of potential side effects, to monitor their health while on medications and to serve as a personal resource for a potentially risky drug. There is no substitution for that.

> "Providing insurance coverage for [over-the-counter] access [to birth control] makes it possible for more women to make and carry out their own decisions about their reproductive lives and health."

# Birth Control Pills Should Be Available over the Counter and Still Covered by Insurance

*Britt Wahlin*

*Britt Wahlin is director of development and communications for Ibis Reproductive Health, an international nonprofit organization dedicated to improving women's reproductive autonomy, choices, and health. In the following viewpoint, Wahlin explains the importance of ensuring that birth control pills are both widely available over the counter and fully covered by insurance. While the Affordable Care Act ensures that birth control pills are covered by insurance, there is still a requirement for a prescription. Prescriptions are difficult to obtain for many women and serve as a barrier to access for them. As women with Medicaid do with emergency contraception and women served by the Brit-*

*ish National Health Service can for birth control pills, all US women should be able to obtain birth control pills at little to no cost. Compared to the costs of unplanned pregnancies incurred by the public and insurance companies, Wahlin concludes, the expense of providing free over-the-counter birth control pills is minimal and makes economic sense.*

As you read, consider the following questions:

1. What groups of women does Wahlin say face the most barriers to getting birth control on time and affordably?

2. According to the author, what is the retail price of emergency contraception?

3. What does a new law in Australia allow pharmacists to do, according to Wahlin?

In February [2013], amidst the ongoing battle over religious employers and no co-pay contraception, the [Barack] Obama administration quietly issued a set of frequently asked questions [FAQ] to shed light on how insurance companies should implement the health reform law's new requirement to cover contraception with no cost sharing. The FAQ makes it crystal clear that insurers must cover the full range of FDA [Food and Drug Administration]-approved contraceptive methods—including IUDs [intrauterine devices], vaginal rings, birth control pills, and even over-the-counter (OTC) contraceptives.

The new HHS [US Department of Health and Human Services] guidance is good news for those of us working to get an over-the-counter birth control pill in the US. When the American College of Obstetricians and Gynecologists recently announced its support for making the pill OTC, one of the concerns expressed was that insurance plans might not cover an OTC pill. The guidance should remove any doubt that a future OTC pill will be covered by insurance. Unfortunately, however, it still falls short by stipulating that a woman must get a prescription in order to use her insurance for OTC contraception.

## Prescriptions Bar Access

Sadly, the prescription requirement defeats the purpose of having an OTC pill in the first place. Research has shown that the prescription requirement is a barrier to many women accessing and using birth control. Studies also show that women who get the pill without a prescription stay on the pill at least as long—and possibly longer—than women who have to get a prescription for refills. Women who are able to get the pill over the counter like the convenience of getting it directly in a pharmacy without a prescription, and they still see their providers for well-woman care.

Being able to pick up your pills at the store, without needing a prescription or paying additional costs, would provide relief for many women, particularly those who currently face the most barriers to getting the birth control they need on time and affordably. Young women, women of color, and immigrant women face a whole slew of obstacles both to getting their hands on a prescription and to paying out of pocket for contraception—from lack of health insurance and language barriers, to stigma and poverty. A fully covered OTC pill would knock out some of the most formidable of these.

In the case of emergency contraception—which a federal court recently ruled should be made available OTC to all women with no restrictions—we know that many women cannot afford the $30 to $50 retail price, so insurance coverage is hugely important. But having to get a prescription in order to get that insurance coverage adds unnecessary delays to accessing this time-sensitive medication.

## Medicaid Provides a Model

So how can we get insurance to cover over-the-counter birth control pills—and other OTC contraceptive methods—without requiring a prescription? In fact, some states are already doing this through their Medicaid programs, using their own funds to cover over-the-counter emergency contraception without requiring a prescription. A woman can walk into a pharmacy, show her Medicaid card, and walk out with emergency contraception without paying anything. Across the Atlantic, the British National Health Service is covering birth control pills without a prescription as part of a pilot project in several London pharmacies. And in Australia, a new law allows pharmacists to dispense a pack of birth control pills to women who previously had the medication prescribed by a doctor but whose prescription has expired.

An OTC pill would be good for women because it would expand the ways they are able to access contraception and give them more control over their health. Women who run out of their prescribed pills or forget to bring them on vacation may find an OTC pill to be a critical stopgap. An OTC pill could also be an important option for women who will remain uninsured after 2014, as well as for the women employed by religious organizations that refuse to provide contraceptive coverage. And some insured women might prefer to pay a small amount for the convenience of getting the pill quickly at the pharmacy, rather than taking time off from work or school to visit their health provider. It's also important to mention that an OTC pill, next to the condoms and spermicides on the drugstore shelf, would be the most effective contraceptive method ever sold over the counter in the US.

## Covered OTC Access Makes Sense

No-co-pay contraception and over-the-counter birth control pills and other OTC methods make sense. From a public health perspective, these things could help reduce unintended pregnancy. Covering contraception without requiring a prescription also makes sense from the perspective of the insurance company's bottom line: birth control is cheap, while an unplanned birth is not. Perhaps most importantly, providing insurance coverage for OTC access without restrictions makes it possible for more women to make and carry out their own decisions about their reproductive lives and health.

Making contraception as available, accessible, and affordable as possible is good for women. Ultimately, ensuring that insurers will cover OTC birth control without requiring a prescription is another critical step on the path to making that goal a reality.

# Periodical and Internet Sources Bibliography

*The following articles have been selected to supplement the diverse views presented in this chapter.*

| | |
|---|---|
| David W. Freeman | "Are Mammography Guidelines Making Breast Cancer Deadlier?," CBS News, May 2, 2011. www.cbsnews.com. |
| Amanda Hess | "Put the Pill on Drugstore Shelves. Pregnancy Is More Dangerous than Birth Control," *Slate*, April 23, 2013. www.slate.com. |
| Amanda Marcotte | "Time to Demand All Birth Control Pills Be Sold over the Counter," RH Reality Check, May 5, 2013. http://rhrealitycheck.org. |
| Melinda Wenner Moyer | "Drug Problem: Women Aren't Properly Represented in Scientific Studies," *Slate*, July 28, 2010. www.slate.com. |
| Rebecca Peck | "Over the Counter Oral Contraceptives Are Bad for Women's Health," Truth and Charity Forum, December 17, 2012. www.truthandcharityforum.org. |
| Genevra Pittman | "Most Women Back Over-the-Counter Birth Control Pills," Reuters, May 2, 2013. www.reuters.com. |
| Karen Springen | "Breakthroughs in Women's Health," *Chicago*, January 20, 2011. |
| USA Today | "Birth Control Pill Proposal Not Easy to Take," November 29, 2012. |
| Jacque Wilson | "Physicians: Birth Control Should Be Sold Without a Prescription," CNN, November 21, 2012. www.cnn.com. |

OPPOSING
VIEWPOINTS®
SERIES

CHAPTER 4

# What Are Key Health Issues That Affect US Servicewomen?

# Chapter Preface

A ctive duty military women face many health challenges that civilian women do not. This is not surprising given their often harsh living conditions, but the high rates of unintended pregnancy (16.29 percent versus 7 percent among civilian women), sexually transmitted infections (seven times the rate of civilian women), and binge drinking (33 percent, versus 6–7 percent of civilian women), coupled with the low rate of contraceptive use (33 percent of unmarried active duty women) were surprising to many when a paper was released in 2012 reporting these results. Study lead author Vinita Goyal states, "A qualitative study of women enlisted in the Navy revealed potential barriers to condom use while in the military. These women reported feeling stigmatized as promiscuous if they requested condoms and believed their male counterparts to be exempt from the same criticism. They also reported not using condoms because if found this would be evidence of violation of the policy prohibiting sexual activity while deployed." Goyal recommends greater awareness of these high risk behaviors and threats to reproductive health among all health care providers, both within and outside the Department of Defense, to better meet the health needs of military women.

Toward this end, the American College of Obstetricians and Gynecologists released a committee opinion on military women and veterans that echoed Goyal's study results, and made the following recommendations for women's reproductive health care providers:

1. Assess women for history of military service and inquire about Veteran status

2. Understand reproductive health risks of military service

3. Be knowledgeable about preconception care, family planning, and contraceptive considerations for deployed women and women Veterans

4. Screen for interpersonal violence, including military sexual trauma

5. Promote a research agenda that studies the effect of military status on reproductive health

6. Engage with the local Veterans Health Administration facility and other entities that serve Veterans.

Given that the ban on women serving in combat was lifted in 2013, the health risks they encounter will only increase, and research into the extent of these risks and how women respond to service is sparse. To better meet the health care needs of military women during and outside of deployment, health researchers have formed the Consortium on the Health and Readiness of Servicewomen (CHARS), which includes both private and public researchers who specialize in epidemiology, neurocognitive psychology, nursing, and family studies from the Naval Health Research Center (NHRC) in San Diego, from universities, the government, and private institutions. The goal of CHARS is to raise awareness of current studies and encourage collaboration among researchers to produce new studies. Stephanie McWhorter, a research psychologist with the NHRC, said in a statement: "We want to encourage people to engage in more collaborative, multidisciplinary research so we can produce findings that can help the Defense Department."

Various health issues faced by military women are debated by the authors in the following chapter.

"*[Department of Defense] components have taken positive steps toward addressing the female-specific health care needs of deployed servicewomen.*"

# The Department of Defense Has Made Progress on Providing Health Care for Deployed Servicewomen

## US Government Accountability Office

*The US Government Accountability Office (GAO) is an independent, nonpartisan agency that works for Congress, investigating how the federal government spends taxpayer dollars. In the following viewpoint, the GAO reports that, overall, the health care provided to US servicewomen during deployments is generally adequate, in all areas except the prevention of and response to sexual assault. Servicewomen receive health screenings prior to deployment, and gender-specific care is provided to them during deployment. The variety of women's health care services varies based on the area of deployment or the size of the naval vessel or base. Most of the women surveyed by the authors expressed satisfaction with their medical care during deployment. The au-*

"Military Personnel: DOD Has Taken Steps to Meet the Health Needs of Deployed Servicewomen, but Actions Are Needed to Enhance Care for Sexual Assault Victims," GAO-13-182, Report to Congressional Addressees, January 29, 2013.

*thors conclude that robust training is needed at all levels within the Department of Defense in the areas of sexual assault prevention and response in order to fully meet the needs of US servicewomen (and men) who are sexually assaulted during active duty.*

As you read, consider the following questions:

1. What is the postpartum deferment period for women serving in the US Navy, according to the GAO?

2. As reported by the author, how many facilities in Afghanistan were providing Role-1 level care in November 2012?

3. How many of the ninety-two servicewomen interviewed by the GAO indicated they did not feel the medical and mental health needs of servicewomen were being met during deployment?

DOD [The US Department of Defense] has developed policies and guidance that include female-specific aspects to help address the health care needs of female servicemembers during deployment. Prior to deploying, servicewomen are screened for potentially deployment-limiting conditions. According to DOD officials and health care providers with whom we met, such pre-screening helps ensure that many female-specific health care needs are addressed prior to deployment. Further, DOD components have conducted reviews of the health care needs of servicewomen during deployments. DOD also collects health care data on the medical services provided to deployed servicewomen in Afghanistan and aboard Navy vessels.

## DOD Policies and Guidance

DOD components have put in place policies and guidance that include female-specific aspects to help address the health care needs of servicewomen during deployment. DOD and service officials told us that while the department's policies are generally gender-neutral and focus on addressing the health care needs of all servicemembers, some of the policies and guidance include female-specific aspects such as pregnancy, pelvic examinations, and screening mammography. In certain instances, the services' policies reflect clinical practice guidelines that come from outside the department, such as those from the American College of Obstetricians and Gynecologists. For example, we found that the Army changed its pre-deployment screening requirements due to a change in American College of Obstetricians and Gynecologists guidelines for cervical cytology [cell] screening. Additionally, we found that Navy guidelines require the provision of standbys—individuals who could be present during sensitive or potentially compromising physical examinations—during medical examinations when female genitalia or breasts are exposed or examined by a medical provider, in accordance with Joint Commission [on Hospital Accreditation] guidelines.

According to DOD and service officials, although there may be some gender differences for particular diagnoses, behavioral health care services—that is, mental health care and substance abuse counseling—are not gender-specific. The treatment of servicemembers' behavioral health care needs and the availability of services to treat those needs, therefore, do not vary based on gender.

## Pre-deployment Screening

DOD has established a medical tracking system for assessing the medical condition of servicemembers to help ensure that only those who are medically and mentally fit are deployed outside of the United States. According to service officials and health care providers with whom we met, pre-deployment screenings help ensure that many women's health care needs are addressed prior to deployment. As part of DOD's pre-deployment screening process, servicemembers of both sexes are screened for potentially deployment-limiting medical conditions that would render them unsuitable to perform their duties during deployment. Servicemembers of both sexes are also required to complete a pre-deployment health assessment questionnaire. DOD requires that servicemembers' questionnaires be reviewed by a health care provider to determine whether the servicemember is fit to deploy. Service officials we spoke with told us that this screening also provides servicemembers an opportunity to discuss and address with a health care provider any health concerns they may have prior to deploying. The officials said they rely on the questionnaires, reviews of servicemembers' medical records, and physical examinations to identify an individual's health care needs prior to deployments.

Some deployment-limiting conditions are female-specific: for example, each of the military services defines pregnancy as a deployment-limiting condition. Each of the services has also established a postpartum deferment period—6 months for the Army, the Air Force, and the Marine Corps, and 12 months for the Navy. During this period, servicewomen are not required to deploy or redeploy, so as to enable mothers to recover from childbirth and to bond with their children. However, each of the military services has a policy that allows servicewomen to voluntarily deploy before the period has expired. Typically, during deployment servicewomen who are confirmed to be pregnant may not remain deployed. For example, servicewomen who are confirmed to be pregnant in Afghanistan may not remain in theater and must notify their military chain of command or supervisor immediately. They are required to be redeployed within 14 days of receipt of notification. Navy guidance prohibits a pregnant servicewoman from remaining aboard a vessel if the time required to transport her to emergency obstetric and gynecological care exceeds 6 hours. Servicewomen who are confirmed to be pregnant at sea are to be sent at the earliest opportunity to the closest shore-based U.S. military facility that can provide obstetric and gynecological care. Navy medical providers we met with during our site visits stated that pregnant servicewomen are typically transferred off the vessel within days of confirmation of their pregnancy. Further, we found that female-specific deployment-limiting conditions sometimes depend on the deployed environment: for example, women with conditions such as recurrent pelvic pain or abnormal vaginal bleeding are disqualified from submarine service. . . .

## A Variety of Health Care Services

The health care services, and in turn the female-specific health care services available to deployed servicewomen, vary depending on the deployed environment. DOD provides three levels of health service support to servicemembers deployed to Afghanistan. The most basic level of care is provided at "Role 1" facilities, which include primary care facilities and outpatient clinics. "Role 2" facilities provide advanced trauma management and emergency medical treatment. The highest level of care that DOD provides in Afghanistan is at "Role 3" facilities. These facilities are equivalent to full-spectrum hospitals and are staffed and equipped to provide resuscitation, initial wound surgery, and post-operative treatment. As of November 2012, there were 143 facilities in Afghanistan providing Role-1 level care, 24 facilities providing Role-2 level care, and 5 facilities providing Role-3 level care. According to senior medical officials with U.S. Forces Afghanistan and the International Security Assistance Force Joint Command, most gynecological care is provided at Role 1 facilities, and infantry battalions and most forward operating bases and combat outposts in Afghanistan can at a minimum provide Role 1-level care.

We found that servicewomen while deployed at sea have access to providers of primary care, although the health care services that are available aboard Navy vessels largely depend on the type and class of vessel. Larger vessels generally offer a wider range of services—including specialized services—than do smaller vessels, due largely to their more robust crew levels and capabilities. The medical department of an aircraft carrier, for example, typically consists of more than 40 billets [living quarters], including a family practitioner, a physician's assistant, and a clinical psychologist. Similarly, the medical department of a WASP-class amphibious assault ship consists of more than 20 billets, including a medical officer. For cruisers, destroyers, and frigates, the medical department typically consists of only a handful of billets, including an Independent Duty Hospital Corpsman, but no medical officer. For Ohio-class submarines, the sole source of medical care aboard is an Independent Duty Hospital Corpsman. Each of these classes of vessels is capable of providing health care services to servicemembers of both sexes.

## Care in Afghanistan

At the 15 selected locations we visited in Afghanistan and Navy vessels, health care providers and servicewomen told us that the health care services available to deployed servicemembers generally meet the needs of servicewomen. Health care providers we spoke with in Afghanistan and aboard Navy vessels told us they were capable of providing a wide range of female-specific health care services—including treating certain gynecological conditions such as urinary tract infections and conducting clinical breast examinations—that women might seek while deployed. They also told us that servicemembers had access at least to basic mental health care services. Some female-specific services—such as treatment for an abnormal PAP smear [a test for cervical cancer] result, or mammography services—were not always available, but providers told us that conditions resulting in the need for more specialized services were routinely addressed prior to deployment. For example, providers with an expeditionary medical group we met in Afghanistan told us that in their experience PAP smears are rarely performed in theater except for women who had received abnormal PAP smear results prior to deploying and needed follow-up checks after 6 months. Those providers also told us that screening mammography is not provided in theater because screening mammography is generally preventative care, which is conducted as part of a woman's annual exam prior to deployment. Health care providers from multiple Navy vessels we visited also told us that a number of female-specific health care services—from performing PAP smears to treating patients with abnormal PAP smear results to mammography services—were not needed during deployments at sea because such services were provided prior to deploying.

According to health care officials and providers with whom we met, women who developed acutely urgent conditions during deployments, to include female-specific conditions, would typically be transferred to a locale offering access to more specialized services. Health care providers with whom we met were able to identify their available options for referring individuals with acutely urgent conditions for specialized care elsewhere if necessary—in Afghanistan, typically, to a higher level of care; during deployments at sea, to another vessel or a shore-based facility. Providers also noted that in some cases they could consult with other health care providers if necessary, including providers specializing in women's health care. For example, at one Role 1 facility we visited in Afghanistan, health care providers noted that their Deputy Command Surgeon specialized in obstetrics and gynecology and was available to consult on cases if they needed assistance. As another example, Navy Independent Duty Hospital Corpsmen told us that they could consult with their physician supervisor if necessary during deployments at sea.

At each of the locations we visited we found that a variety of steps were being taken to help ensure that servicewomen had a reasonable amount of privacy during examinations as well. For example, each of the locations we visited offered at a minimum a medical examination room with privacy curtains that could be drawn. In most instances, doors with locks were available as well. We also observed that signs could be posted indicating that an examination was in process. Further, health care providers told us that a standby—individuals who could be present during sensitive or potentially compromising physical examinations—was available at each location we visited. . . .

## Results of Servicewomen Interviews

Based on information provided by the 92 servicewomen we interviewed at selected locations in Afghanistan and aboard Navy vessels, the responses from 60 indicated that they felt the medical and mental health needs of women were generally being met during deployments, whereas the responses from 8 indicated they did not feel the medical and mental health needs of women were generally being met during deployments. The responses from an additional 8 servicewomen suggested that they had a mixed opinion as to whether the medical and mental health needs of women were being met during deployments, and 16 told us they did not know or did not have an opinion. Servicewomen who indicated during our interviews that the medical and mental health needs of women were generally being met during deployments offered a variety of reasons for their responses. At one location we visited in Afghanistan, a female Airman told us that if she had a health problem, the medical facility at her location could treat her or send her elsewhere if needed. She further noted that if the problem were serious enough she could be evacuated. Similarly, a female Army soldier we met at another location told us she felt some of the best care that she has received in her life has been military health care. At another location, a female Marine told us that the care provided to her was as good as she could imagine, given the operating environment. Aboard one Navy vessel we visited, a female sailor told us that even though mental health care was not available aboard her ship, it was available ashore, and the ship could handle emergencies at sea.

Servicewomen we interviewed who indicated that they felt the medical and mental health needs of women were generally not being met during deployments offered a variety of reasons for their responses as well. At one location we visited in Afghanistan, a female airman told us that she believed the military was trying to meet the health needs of women, but still had work to do—noting, for example, that a medication she was prescribed had given her yeast infections. At another, a female Army soldier told us that she had experienced difficulty obtaining sleep medication. In the case of deployments at sea, one female sailor expressed concern that a mental health provider was not aboard. Of servicewomen who offered a mixed opinion, one female sailor told us that she felt junior health care providers were limited in the types of procedures they could perform and lacked practical experience.

## Sexual Assault Victims

DOD has taken steps to address the provision of medical and mental health care for servicemembers who are sexually assaulted, but several factors affect the extent to which this care is available. Specifically, the branch of military service and the operational uncertainties of a deployed environment can affect the ready availability of medical and mental health care services for victims of sexual assault. Additionally, care is in some cases affected because military health care providers do not have a consistent understanding of their responsibilities in caring for sexual assault victims who make restricted reports of sexual assault. Further, first responders such as Sexual Assault Response Coordinators and Victim Advocates are not always aware of the specific health care services available to sexual assault victims at their respective locations. . . .

## Sexual Assault Victims Lack Support

As women continue to assume an expanding and evolving role in the military it is important that DOD be well positioned to meet the health care needs of deployed servicewomen and ensure their readiness. To the department's credit, DOD components have taken positive steps toward addressing the female-specific health care needs of deployed servicewomen, and we note that at the selected locations we visited during the course of our review the responses from most servicewomen we spoke with indicated that they felt the medical and mental health needs of women were generally being met during deployments. DOD also has taken positive steps in making medical and mental health care services available to sexual assault victims of both sexes. However, DOD's limited health care guidance on the restricted sexual assault reporting option and first responders' inconsistent knowledge about available resources are factors that affect the quality and availability of that care. Left unaddressed, such factors can undermine DOD's efforts to address the problem of sexual assault in the military by eroding servicemembers' confidence in the department's programs and decreasing the likelihood that victims of sexual assault will turn to the programs or seek care and treatment when needed.

## Training Is Needed

To help ensure that sexual assault victims have consistent access to health care services and the reporting options specified in DOD's sexual assault prevention and response policies, we recommend that the Secretary of Defense direct the Under Secretary of Defense for Personnel and Readiness to direct the Assistant Secretary of Defense for Health Affairs to develop and implement department-level guidance on the provision of medical and mental health care to victims of sexual assault that specifies health care providers' responsibilities to respond to and care for sexual assault victims, whether in the United States or in deployed environments.

To help ensure that Sexual Assault Response Coordinators, Victim Advocates, and health care personnel have a consistent understanding of the medical and mental health resources available at their respective locations for sexual assault victims, we recommend that the Secretary of Defense direct the Under Secretary of Defense for Personnel and Readiness, in collaboration with the military departments, to take steps to improve compliance regarding the completion of annual refresher training on sexual assault prevention and response.

*"The Services must ensure all of our Service Members are healthy, protected warriors regardless of gender."*

# Better Provisions for Specialized Care Are Needed for Deployed Servicewomen

### Women's Health Assessment Team

*The Women's Health Assessment Team is a special unit within the Health Service Support Assessment Team, International Security Assistance Force, Joint Command (IJC) in Afghanistan. In the following viewpoint, the authors report that greater attention must be paid to educating servicewomen about steps they can take to avoid such common health problems as urinary tract infections and vaginitis during deployment. The authors recommend that women be given training and equipment to test and diagnose themselves for routine ailments to improve their willingness and their ability to access care, such as antibiotics for urinary tract infections. They also recommend that commanding officers receive education to increase their awareness of female-specific health challenges during deployment and the solutions to these issues. The authors also assert that sexual assault is a seri-*

"The Concerns of Women Currently Serving in the Afghanistan Theater of Operations," White Paper. ISAF Joint Command, October 10, 2011, pp. 7–9. 11–12, 28, 30–31. Copyright © 2011 by NATO.

*ous problem and a major concern for deployed servicewomen. They provide a number of recommendations for improving sexual assault prevention and response in the military.*

As you read, consider the following questions:

1. How many women from all services have deployed in support of operations in the Middle East, according to the authors?

2. What percentage of women were hesitant to utilize sick call during deployment, according to a study cited by the authors?

3. What is the estimated prevalence of sexual assault in the military, according to the Women's Health Assessment Team?

Women have participated in America's military efforts since the Revolutionary War. Their roles have evolved from supportive in nature to those with direct assignment in the war zone since WWII [World War II]. More recently, with the legislative changes during the first Gulf War [in 1991], over 90% of roles are open to women. Today [2011], almost 275,000 women from all Services have deployed in support of contingency operations in the Middle East that encompass the full dimensions of the battle space. Female Service Members are assigned to units and positions that may necessitate combat actions, like those assigned to our female engagement teams. They are fully prepared to respond, and to succeed, as they have in both Iraq and Afghanistan. The Services must ensure all of our Service Members are healthy, protected warriors regardless of gender. Deployment in support of military operations imposes unique conditions of daily living on military women that have an impact on health and wellness. This report reviews the major themes derived from the voices of female Service Members currently serving in the Afghanistan Theater of Operations and leverages existing data to set forth recommendations to ensure that the health of all Service Members is optimized for maximal combat power.

During the Health Service Support (HSS) Assessment of the Afghanistan Theater of Operations, women's concerns were heard at Town Hall meetings held at 10 locations across the Theater. The HSS Team traveled to Role 1, Role 2 and Role 3 facilities throughout the CJOA-A [Coalition Joint Operations Area-Afghanistan]. The team members assessing Women's Health areas consisted of Nurse Corps Officers, an OB/GYN [Obstetrics and Gynecology] Physician, a Pediatrician, and a Medical Service Corps officer. In total, there were over 150 female Service Member participants. Open discussion was encouraged without limitation on the issues. All of the discussions were non-attributional [anonymous], which allowed females of all ranks and services across Afghanistan to have a free and open voice. Surveys that had questions on women's health issues surrounding deployment were also distributed to females after the Town Hall meeting and were returned directly to the HSS team electronically, maintaining confidentiality of the participants.

## Servicewomen Need Better Education

An overarching theme of the HSS Assessment findings is that there is a lack of consistent and timely education for women's health issues and how they are impacted by deployment. Major topics identified by the participants in the Town Hall Meetings included the lack of education on birth control, menstrual cycle control, and feminine hygiene during deployment. This lack of education and counseling is evidenced by utilization practices in Theater. A Force Health Protection Assessment reported a 3% higher utilization rate for female genitourinary encounters during Operation Iraqi Freedom (OIF)/Operation Enduring Freedom (OEF) than in garrison [at military bases] from January 2005 to July 2007. It is not surprising that deployment conditions impact the prevalence of common women's health conditions. Correlations have been found between field conditions, feminine hygiene practices, and reported urinary tract infections (UTI) and vaginitis symptoms. UTI, vaginitis, and menstrual symptoms are the most common gynecologic health problems for the women serving in current conflicts. Risk factors for UTI in the deployed environment include impaired voiding and impaired feminine hygiene, which are fostered by poor sanitation conditions, lack of latrines, lack of privacy, and the inconvenience of undressing in full battle gear. The risk is compounded by women intentionally drinking less fluid to avoid the need to urinate and postponing/delaying urination.

While more often than not, female Soldiers continue to drive on with their mission, there is evidence that the symptoms of menstrual disorders and infections can impact mission readiness. Forty-eight percent of the women in one anonymous study of nearly 850 women reported that symptoms of vaginitis and UTIs compromised their duties during deployments, and 27% reported lost duty time due to their symptoms. Similarly, military women perceive that menstrual symptoms affect performance of duties in the field setting and contributed to lost duty days during deployments to OIF/OEF. Appropriate counseling on menstrual cycle control, contraception, and urogenital hygiene could reduce the utilization of healthcare and disruption in mission readiness.

Participants agreed that more education would be helpful and favored education being provided as routine training throughout the Soldier life cycle, starting with basic training and continuing over time, with further opportunities for discussion and counseling on the topics during the Periodic Health Assessment (PHA). There was limited support for including women's health education in pre-deployment training, where it would compete with other time-consuming training demands. Women also noted the importance of educating their male peers and leaders but believed learning would be best facilitated in single-sex groups. Recommendations for education are given priority in this report, since education early in the Soldier life cycle will provide the foundation of self-care required to decrease the risks of menstrual disorders, urogenital infections, and unwanted pregnancy, ultimately enhancing mission readiness.

## Preventive Practices Recommended

Incorporate the prevention and self-diagnosis of vaginitis and urinary tract infections, as well as education on menstrual disorders, contraception, urogenital hygiene, and menstrual cycle control into the Program of Instruction (POI) for Initial Entry Training (IET), Advanced Training (AIT) and Officer and NCO [noncommissioned officers] development courses. While personal hygiene for all Soldiers is already included in the POI for IET, there is a limited amount of gender-specific issues; the majority of female-specific training is focused on the prevention of sexually transmitted infections. We therefore recommend that more gender-specific hygiene and self-care education for females be added to the POIs. Training should also include instruction on specific self-care practices that women can use to moderate the effects of deployment on their genitourinary health, including the use and benefits of the FUDD [feminine urinary diversion devices]. Educational modules and printed materials should be packaged for Soldiers and leaders, as well as for export and utilization by our sister Services. The additional education in the POI should be delivered to both male and female Soldiers, although we recommend that it is offered in single-sex settings to encourage discussion and increased comprehension of the topics. Including the material in education sessions for males will improve their comprehension of women's health issues and foster respect among members of a unit. This training will increase awareness of women's health issues, improve sensitivity to gender specific issues and foster an expectation of respect. Additionally this knowledge will prepare males for leadership positions in which they will be responsible for ensuring the well-being of all members of their unit, including those with female health issues. Our assessment revealed that leaders desire the knowledge about the issues that affect their female Soldiers, particularly in relationship to an impending deployment. Therefore, we recommend leaders also receive specific deployment-related information on women's health issues during pre-deployment health briefings, which has been well-received at the Division level. . . .

## Difficulties in Seeking Care

Women's health issues are compounded by the findings that many women hesitate to seek medical care when they have a female health concern. The reasons cited at the Town Hall meetings included having to be seen by a male provider, who may be either in her chain of command or someone she works with on a daily basis. Well designed studies have supported these findings on a much larger scale and across Services. One study of 841 service women found that nearly 50% of the women (411) were hesitant to utilize sick call during deployment and 25% stated that they would not even go. When specifically asked about seeking care for genitourinary symptoms, 69% of women reported that their provider was a medic or corpsman and their concerns were lack of confidence, as well as cleanliness and privacy of healthcare facilities. This suggests that many female Service Members do not have a good understanding of how to access a licensed provider in our healthcare system. This finding also supports the need for more education as well as the need to empower women to take an educated role in the mitigation, prevention, and self-diagnosis for these conditions, where appropriate.

In response to the barriers to seeking care, researchers investigated the use of self-tests to diagnose and treat both vaginitis and urinary tract infection, thereby avoiding the need for a healthcare visit for a gynecologic exam. When women at the Town Hall meetings were presented with the idea of doing their own self-test and diagnosis for vaginitis and urinary tract infections, there was overwhelming support. Experts who have conducted a ten-year program of research have developed a self-test kit that has been validated against diagnostic gold standards in a series of investigations, including with a military population. The kit that was tested included point-of-care testing devices for determining bacterial vaginosis or a yeast infection and/or a UTI, a thermometer, and the Women in the Military Self-Diagnosis (WMSD ©) decision-making algorithm. Education included use of the kit, a video, and scenario-based use of the decision-making guide.

## Self Care Is Beneficial

In preliminary analysis of data (unpublished) from the most recent of the series, the diagnostic accuracy of the testing devices with the decision-making guide for bacterial vaginosis and yeast infections approaches that of clinical diagnoses by a provider. Furthermore, it appears to lead to accurate self treatment with oral medications, as well (unpublished data). This team also found when military women reported the classic triad of symptoms for a UTI, diagnosis both by the self-testing device and by a clinical provider were not as accurate as diagnosis by the gold standard culture; yet it is important to note that it is common practice to diagnose UTI and prescribe treatment over the telephone, based on reported *symptoms* only, without a culture. Therefore, the use of the self-test kit in combination with the presence of UTI symptoms is seen as a feasible alternative to a clinic visit, with similar outcomes.

It is the opinion of the subject matter experts conducting this program of research that the kit provides a feasible method for women to provide self-care and thus seek appropriate treatment without the unnecessary step of a clinician visit. Self-testing and diagnosis of UTIs and vaginitis could reduce the time women spend seeking healthcare and increase mission readiness. Not seeking healthcare, nor performing self-care testing for these conditions, could result in no treatment or inappropriate self-treatment and development of more serious complications, such as kidney or pelvic infections. In these cases, the burden on the healthcare system is increased and mission readiness is severely compromised. Given the low risk associated with the testing and low potential for misdiagnoses, in combination with the potential benefits of decreased burden on the healthcare system, it is our recommendation to pursue the development of a women's self-diagnosis kit. . . .

## Sexual Assault Is a Serious Problem

Sexual assault is clearly not a gender specific issue as it affects male and female victims and its impact extends much broader to affect unit cohesion and degrade mission readiness. Prevention and intervention efforts also cannot be gender focused as the solutions are team based. . . . Sexual assault in the military is defined as "intentional sexual contact, characterized by use of force, threats, intimidation, abuse of authority, or when the victim does not or cannot consent." The prevalence of sexual assault in the military services has been estimated at 9.5% to 33%, however true prevalence is hampered by the phenomenon of underreporting (estimated to be <10% of true occurrence), various definitions of sexual assault, and the lack of consistent reporting systems in the military. . . .

The literature is clear that Service Members who experience sexual assault exhibit deleterious psychological and physical health effects including higher rates of depression and post traumatic stress symptoms, poor emotional functioning, and substance abuse. Our DoD population has several risk factors for experiencing higher than average rates of sexual assault than the general population. Risk factors in the DoD include a younger population with a smaller proportion of women to men, and a higher rate of Service Members with prior sexual victimizations and prior perpetrations as compared to the civilian population. Environmental factors in garrison and while deployed that increase the risk for sexual assault include solitary duty (especially at night), poor barracks security, and insufficient environmental lighting. . . .

## Barriers to Reporting Assault

During our assessment, barriers to reporting sexual assault were also clearly vocalized. Concerns included a lack of trust in the fidelity of the reporting system and the confidentiality processes in place. Women conveyed fears of becoming "the talk of the unit," that the report would be turned around to reflect negatively on them, and that reporting would cause additional suffering without likelihood that the perpetrator would be punished. This echoes the findings of larger studies which show that barriers to reporting include shame/ embarrassment, the stigma and social consequences associated with sexual assault, fear of reprisal, mistrust of the process, and characteristics of the perpetrator, in particular if the perpetrator is a Family member, friend, coworker, or higher rank than the victim.

Lastly, a common theme that was heard from women across the CJOA-A was that while they generally felt safe, they noted a lack of simple physical security measures such as locks and lighting. For example, female sleeping tents commonly have locking doors on one end and just a zipper on the other end. The lack of security measures was reconfirmed during the recent (May 2011) SHARP ATO [Sexual Harassment/Assault Response and Prevention Afghanistan Theater of Operations] Assessment Team visit, which led them to recommend "immediate application of locks to living quarters, showers, and latrines; noting that cipher lock codes should be changed every 90 days." The team recommended that "with consideration to blackout conditions, commanders should consider improved outdoor lighting on every FOB [Forward Operating Base]." The SHARP assessment team also recommended that the battle buddy system should be highly encouraged. Many women we interviewed expressed that their male counterparts are protective of the . . . females and actively ensure that women are not in vulnerable situations. Some groups from larger installations discussed feeling harassed by local nationals or Third Country Nationals—this included "cat-calling," staring at, or ignoring women.

The Military is steeped in tradition and is built on a foundation of unshakable values. The Army Values of Loyalty, Duty, Respect, Selfless Service, Honor, Integrity and Personal Courage combined with a Warrior Ethos to never leave a comrade will be the keys to combating sexual assault within our ranks. Pursuant to the HSS Assessment Team's observations and analysis of field notes, the following recommendations are made in an effort to capitalize on the participants' suggestions and dovetail with DoD recommendations and strategy.

## Measures to Enhance Prevention

*Require Installations Assess Physical Safety Measures.* Improve physical security and monitoring on lodging and bathroom facilities. Improve lighting where tactically acceptable on Forward Operating Bases.

*Review Theater Policy Regarding Distribution of SAFE Providers.* Enhance competence, effectiveness, and consider the use of a regional strategy.

*Convene a Team of Experts from the Tri-Services.* Fully investigate the integration of Service policies on sexual assault prevention and response programs in Theater, including the training of SAFE providers, Sexual Assault Response Coordinators, and Victim Advocates.

*Professionalize the VA Roles.* Provide national certification and continuing education for Victim Advocates.

*Leverage and Synergize with Comprehensive Soldier Fitness.* Target interpersonal skills, self esteem, assertiveness and the core values which will enhance a culture of trust, respect and unity of members.

*Ensure 100% Implementation of the SHARP Program.* Collaborate with HQDA G-1 to track objective SHARP implementation and outcome measures of effectiveness.

| "Women, although less likely than men to be exposed to a traumatic event, are much more likely to develop [post-traumatic stress disorder]."

# Servicewomen Are More Likely than Servicemen to Develop Post-Traumatic Stress Disorder

*Bari Walsh*

*Bari Walsh is a writer and editor and the director of communications at the Harvard University Graduate School of Arts and Sciences. In the following viewpoint, Walsh reports on the widespread incidence of post-traumatic stress disorder (PTSD) among US women veterans. She traces the evolution of PTSD research and points to various differences in the way in which men and women experience and process trauma, as well as the variances in their symptoms when they do suffer from PTSD. There are many factors that influence women's susceptibility to PTSD, and they likely explain why women in the military are twice as likely as men to develop PTSD. Hormones and neurochemistry play a significant role, she explains. Walsh notes also that researchers indicate that women are additionally vulnerable because they are more often the victims of sexual assault, or Military Sexual Trauma, and personal types of trauma are more psychologically damaging than impersonal trauma such as experienced in combat.*

As you read, consider the following questions:

1. How many women have served in Iraq and Afghanistan since 2001, according to Walsh?

2. According to the author, what year was VA screening for Military Sexual Trauma first mandated?

3. What percentage of women lost their PTSD diagnosis following Cognitive Processing Therapy, according to Patricia Resick's study as cited by Walsh?

Michele Parkinson survived the near-daily bombings in Kirkuk [Iraq]. She managed the blood. She handled the nausea as she picked through the pockets of a corpse, searching for an ID. What she couldn't get through, it turns out, was a trip to the pharmacy back home in Massachusetts.

A sergeant first class in the National Guard, Parkinson had been evacuated from Iraq in 2005, suffering from severe and medically mysterious headaches. When she arrived at Fort Dix, [New Jersey] she thought she was home free. And she felt fine—as long as she was in the company of other soldiers.

On a trip to the National Cemetery in Washington, D.C., she left her group of fellow soldiers to use the restroom. "When I came out of the stall, it seemed like there were a thousand women standing there," she recalls. "It was maybe about 20, I went into a panic, I couldn't breathe, I started shaking, I pushed my way out, and I ended up falling to my knees. When I looked around and saw my soldiers standing there, I calmed right down. That was the beginning of it."

Within days of arriving home, says Parkinson, she started to experience extreme anxiety. One day at her pharmacy, she started to shake, and broke down in tears.

"I just totally lost it," she says. "For 10 days I couldn't walk out my door without breaking down."

## PTSD Prevalence Among Women Veterans

Parkinson is among the 190,000 military women who have served in Iraq and Afghanistan since 2001. And she's among the 20 percent of servicewomen who develop post-traumatic stress disorder (PTSD), a debilitating, life-threatening anxiety disorder that may affect as many as 300,000 veterans of the current wars.

When we hear about military-related PTSD, it's mostly in worst-case scenarios: damaged men doing destructive things when they return from service. But women develop PTSD at more than twice the rate men do. Their suffering, generally quieter, is far less publicized, far less researched, and until recently, far less treated. Before this war [on terror], its primary cause was sexual trauma, not combat trauma. But now, with women returning from combat deployments in greater numbers than ever before in U.S. history, the Department of Veterans Affairs [VA] is scrambling to meet a need whose scope is still unknown.

Much of the research to determine the need and shape a solution is being conducted at the VA's National Center for Post-Traumatic Stress Disorder, many of whose leading investigators are Boston University professors who do their work at the VA Boston Healthcare System in Jamaica Plain.

## The Evolution of Trauma Research and Diagnosis

Post-traumatic stress disorder didn't exist as a diagnosis until 1980, says Terence Keane, a [Boston University] School of Medicine professor of psychiatry, who is the director of the

Behavioral Sciences Division of the National Center for PTSD and who developed many of the most widely used PTSD assessment tools. That's when it was added to the Diagnostic and Statistical Manual of Mental Disorders, thanks to a research push in the 1970s by Keane and other pioneers in the field.

But long before then, medical professionals understood that the effects of trauma added up to a persistent set of symptoms in many thousands of sufferers. Shell shock, battle fatigue, post-Vietnam syndrome: these were a few of the names given to the severe adjustment problems experienced by some veterans of 20th-century wars. As researchers began looking closely at what was happening with Vietnam veterans, others noticed remarkably consistent symptoms in some women who had been sexually assaulted and raped—a condition then called rape trauma syndrome—and in Holocaust survivors, who suffered from what was referred to as KZ syndrome.

"These researchers started to communicate with each other," Keane says, building a body of evidence, for a single diagnosis that wasn't specific to the origin of the traumatic experience.

## Destructive Symptoms

Researchers now believe that 20 to 25 percent of people exposed to a traumatic event will develop PTSD, Keane says. The diagnosis encompasses four types of symptoms: reexperiencing, reliving the trauma through nightmares and flashbacks, sometimes brought on by triggers like a car backfiring; avoidance, compulsively steering clear of places or people even loosely associated with the trauma, working too much, or drinking too much; numbness, a lack of warmth for family members, a lack of trust, a lack of interest in favorite activities; and hyperarousal, a jittery sense of panic, a constant state of alert, trouble sleeping, trouble concentrating, and irritability.

These symptoms can become powerfully destructive. They can lead to substance abuse, broken relationships, unemployment and suicide. And they can result in physical illnesses like obesity, heart disease, and diabetes.

Why some people are resilient in the face of trauma and others are not is a matter of continuing interest. "PTSD appears to develop in people who've had multiple exposures to trauma, and also different kinds of exposure," Keane says. Past trauma is like kindling, providing fuel when new trauma occurs.

Another risk factor, it turns out, is gender. Epidemiological studies in the 1990s helped establish that women, although less likely than men to be exposed to a traumatic event, are much more likely to develop PTSD. The reason is unclear.

## More Women Get PTSD

Patricia Resick and other Boston University researchers in the Women's Health Sciences Division of the National Center for PTSD are looking hard for answers, studying the psychology, psychobiology, and treatment of the disorder in women veterans. Their work is just now starting to fill large gaps in a field where the vast majority of research has been done on men.

One thing they would like to know is why 20 percent of women in the military develop PTSD, compared to only 8 percent of men. Resick, a professor of psychiatry and psychology and the director of the women's division, says that some of it has to do with the kind of trauma women experience.

In general, whether in the military or out, sexual trauma is a more significant risk factor for PTSD than combat or the types of trauma that men generally experience, says Resick. "Combat, car accidents, fights—those are impersonal events," she says. "When women are traumatized, they're often traumatized by people who are supposed to love or protect them." In a military setting, "your commanding officer is an authority figure who is supposed to protect you," she says. "Your fellow officers or soldiers are supposed to have your back. So when one of them attacks you, it's a huge betrayal."

## Military Sexual Trauma

Sexual assault and severe sexual harassment—collectively known as military sexual trauma (MST)—is nearly epidemic in the armed services. Amy Street, a MED [Boston University School of Medicine] assistant professor of psychiatry, who leads a VA support team devoted to the issue, says that VA screenings for MST, mandated since 1992 for every veteran, reveal that 20 percent of servicewomen report sexual assaults or severe, threatening harassment, compared to 1 percent of men. Those numbers, she says. are probably an underestimate. And many women veterans report that the sense of betrayal is compounded—and the trauma and shame intensified—when the chain of command fails to act on a reported incident, minimizes it, or even punishes women who report assaults.

Street recently found that even reservists, those military part-timers who serve two weeks a year and one weekend a month, experience "high and impactful" rates of MST, among both women and men. "So even people who had other lives outside of the military tended to experience a lot of harassment and assault," she says, "and even 10 or 20 years later, those experiences were associated with higher rates of depression, poorer functioning, and higher rates of PTSD."

## Gender Plays a Role

Women may also have a biological susceptibility to PTSD, a theory that Suzanne Pineles, a MED [Boston University] assistant professor of psychiatry, is exploring. Pineles, the clinical coordinator of the VA's Women's Stress Disorder Treatment Team, is working with a $760,000 grant from the VA to see how women's menstrual cycles might affect PTSD—its onset, symptoms, and longevity. Researchers have tended to avoid looking at the psychobiology of PTSD in women, perhaps because the fluctuating hormones of the menstrual cycle have been seen as complicating the picture. These same hormones may be the very keys to understanding the disorder in women.

"Estrogen and progesterone both affect stress-producing hormones and physiological processes associated with PTSD," says Pineles. "In this study, instead of trying to control for it, we're exploring the differences."

To do that, she will use what psychologists call the prepulse inhibition task, which measures how well people are able to "gate," or filter out, irrelevant information. "If you give someone a startle stimulus"—like a mild electric shock—"they'll startle," Pineles says. "But if they have a little warning, almost imperceptible, they'll startle less."

A previous study had suggested that people with PTSD lack a robust ability to gate—to filter out unnecessary information—when compared to people without PTSD. It's also known that healthy women in the luteal phase of their menstrual cycle (when progesterone is spiking) gate less well than women in the early follicular phase (when progesterone is low) or than men. Pineles wants to see how much greater the effect is in women with PTSD, so she'll look at a group of women both with and without the disorder. She'll compare their performances on filtering tests and on fear response tests, measuring hormone levels as she goes. It could be that menstrual phases contribute not only to onset, but to the fact that women maintain PTSD symptoms longer than men.

## Attentional Biases

Pineles has also done cross-gender research into so-called attentional biases, in an effort to team whether PTSD is an overreaction to a trauma or an inability to recover from a trauma.

"If you see a bear, your attention will be drawn to it, because it's threatening." she says. "That's adaptive, but people with anxiety disorders have more of that attentional bias, so they're more drawn to the bear."

Pineles studied Vietnam veterans and a group of women veterans who'd been sexually assaulted, and she found the same effect in both groups: the trouble wasn't that they responded more quickly or dramatically to trauma—it was that they could not disengage from trauma.

"Their attention gets glued" on the traumatic trigger, she says. "It's like they're stuck."

## A Looming PTSD Crisis

Of the 1.6 million service members who have deployed to Iraq and Afghanistan since 2001, at least one in six is at risk of developing PTSD. That's hundreds of thousands of fragile, wounded veterans flooding the VA—or worse, not flooding the VA and self-destructing elsewhere. The Department of Defense has responded to the looming crisis, pledging $25 million over the next five years—its largest PTSD grant ever—to put in place the best treatments for the disorder. One of the two treatments being studied is called cognitive processing therapy (CPT), and it was developed by Resick.

## Cognitive Processing Therapy

"People walk away from traumatic events having shattered any preexisting positive beliefs they might have had about themselves or the world," she says. In CPT, a systematic 12-session program, therapists take their patients through the trauma and attempt to find out what meanings they've assigned it, and where they're getting stuck.

Most people blame themselves, Resick says, because they want to think they had more control over the event than they did. CPT helps people let go of that blame, and it also helps them cope with the reality that "sometimes traumas happen and we can't prevent them," she says. "Bad stuff can happen, and it could happen again, and then people only have the choice of coping or not coping. That idea is so scary for some people that they will go way out of their way not to believe it."

CPT is dramatically successful in treating rape victims and battered women, the populations for whom Resick developed it. In one study, she found that 80 percent of women lost their PTSD diagnosis and had, on average, a 75 percent reduction in symptoms after twelve sessions.

Resick's current project will look at active military personnel and compare CPT's effectiveness in group versus individual treatment. The study could have significant policy ramifications, because many VA hospitals provide only or mostly group treatment.

"If it turns out that groups don't work as well, that will have budgetary implications, and the VA will have to plan accordingly," Resick says. "Group treatment is more cost-effective, and if it turns out that group is as good as individual, then it's justifiable."

Resick is also teaching the therapy to clinicians across the country. "Last year we trained 1,200 therapists, 800 just in the VA," she says. "We'll train another 800 this year, and 800 the year after. There's never been a systematic movement like this, to teach therapists to use evidence-based treatments. The VA has invested in this, and I think we're having an impact."

One big question that remains unanswered involves the experiences of women in combat settings. Women are prohibited by law from serving in direct ground combat troops, but in the Iraq and Afghanistan wars, any deployment is a combat deployment. "This is guerilla war, so anything you do is dangerous," says Amy Street, the specialist in military sexual trauma. She and colleagues at the National Center for PTSD are launching a study that she hopes will provide some of the first solid information on combat-induced trauma in women and on the kinds of MST women experience in war zones. "And the thing we really don't know is how women are doing

## Why Some Women Are at Higher Risk for PTSD

Not all women who experience a traumatic event develop PTSD. Women are more likely to develop PTSD if they:

- Have a past mental health problem (e.g., depression or anxiety)

- Experienced a very severe or life-threatening trauma

- Were sexually assaulted

- Were injured during the event

- Had a severe reaction at the time of the event

- Experienced other stressful events afterwards

- Do not have good social support

*US Department of Veterans' Affairs,*
*"Women, Trauma, and PTSD," February 23, 2012.*

following deployment," she continues. "Because we get asked the question all the time, about whether these direct ground combat positions should be open to women. It's a hot political topic."

## "I Want to Be Like I Was"

National Guard veteran Michele Parkinson, who is not a part of any Boston University research project, is proud of her military service.

She says she loves the camaraderie of the military, and her life still revolves around her National Guard duties. She is taking medication and seeing a counselor, and she says her dog helps her keep calm and focused when she's in a crowd. But she still has days when "my mind is going a thousand different ways." Like a paranoid mob boss, she sits with her back to the wall when she goes to restaurants; she can't stand to have people behind her, people she can't see.

"My doctors tell me this is going to get better, and it has," she says. "But I want to be like I was, and I don't think that's going to happen."

*"Study findings suggest that both expo-sure to combat-related stressors and their associated impact on postdeploy-ment mental health ... may be more similar than different for female and male U.S. service members."*

# Servicewomen Are Not More Likely than Servicemen to Develop Post-Traumatic Stress Disorder

*Dawne Vogt et al.*

*Dawne Vogt and her colleagues are medical researchers in public health in Massachusetts. In the following viewpoint, the authors argue that the common belief that women are more prone to de-velop mental health problems following traumatic events is erro-neous and based on faulty data and assumptions. Because men were far more prone to combat exposure and women were not, research focused exclusively on combat exposure and ignored other dimensions of stress related to deployment to a war zone. Since the numbers of women and men reporting exposure to*

Dawne Vogt et al., "Gender Differences in Combat-Related Stressors and Their Associa-tion With Postdeployment Mental Health in a Nationally Representative Sample of U.S. OEF/OIF Veterans," *Journal of Abnormal Psychology*, vol. 120, no. 4, May 30, 2011, pp. 797–799, 802, 804–805. Reproduced by permission.

*combat have equalized, the authors hypothesized that any gender differences in responding to that exposure would be small. Their study shows that women are not more likely than men to have mental health issues related to combat exposure within a year after deployment and that they are just as resilient as men. The authors conclude that further research should be done to evaluate longer-term effects of combat exposure in both men and women.*

As you read, consider the following questions:

1. How many women had been killed or wounded in action during Operation Enduring Freedom and Operation Iraqi Freedom by 2009, according to Vogt and colleagues?

2. As reported by the authors, what percentage of women Operation Enduring Freedom and Operation Iraqi Freedom veterans reported experiencing some level of combat exposure?

3. Why do the authors suggest that policies barring women from ground combat roles may be less meaningful?

As a consequence of women's changing role in the war zone, as well as the evolving nature of modern warfare, female service members have experienced unprecedented levels of combat exposure in the U.S. wars in Afghanistan (Operation Enduring Freedom; OEF) and Iraq (Operation Iraqi Freedom; OIF). While women are still officially barred from direct ground combat positions in the U.S. military, they serve in a variety of positions that put them at risk for combat exposure. Women's risk for combat is compounded by the enemy's increased use of guerilla warfare tactics in recent wars. As of 2009, more than 750 women had been wounded or killed in action during OEF/OIF.

# A Relatively New Phenomenon

Although other countries have employed women in combat roles at different points throughout history (e.g., Russian Women's Battalions of Death during World War I), women's exposure to combat is a relatively new phenomenon in the U.S. As such, this topic has received a great deal of attention in the popular media. However, it has received surprisingly little empirical attention. Moreover, though the literature on the deployment experiences and postdeployment health of OEF/OIF veterans continues to grow, most studies include few women and do not report gender-based analyses. To our knowledge, no published study has yet examined gender differences in exposure to different dimensions of combat-related stress and their associated consequences for postdeployment mental health in a nationally representative sample of U.S. OEF/OIF veterans.

Although anecdotal accounts indicate that female OEF/OIF service members have experienced combat exposure at rates that are much higher than prior U.S. wars, the extent to which the nature and severity of women's combat experiences parallel men's experiences is currently unknown. As one might expect due to women's exclusion from ground combat positions, studies that have reported relevant results generally reveal higher levels of combat exposure for men. However, these differences appear to be quite modest. For example, 45% of women and 50% of men in a national sample of U.S. OEF/OIF veterans reported experiencing some level of combat exposure. Another study that addressed gender differences in a sample of Iraq-deployed combat support troops found that men were more likely to report being in firefights (47% versus 36%) and shooting at the enemy (15% versus 7%), but women were more likely to report handling human remains (38% and 29%). Though these studies suggest substantial levels of combat exposure for OEF/OIF deployed women, an in-depth evaluation of gender differences in the nature and severity of combat exposure in this cohort has not yet been conducted.

Women's increased exposure to combat also raises the question of whether there may be gender differences in the mental health consequences of combat exposure. Though the broader literature indicates that women are at higher risk for mental health problems following a variety of traumatic events, most of this literature is based on noncombat traumas (e.g., motor vehicle accidents, assaults, etc). Moreover, although gender differences appear smaller when analyses are restricted to combat trauma samples, the literature that is currently available is based on prior cohorts in which women's combat exposure was limited, and thus, may not allow for a robust test of this hypothesis. In addition, most prior studies on gender differences in combat trauma have relied on analyses that do not directly evaluate gender differences in associations between combat exposure and postdeployment mental health. As a consequence, there is little evidence to inform conclusions regarding the extent to which women and men differ in their vulnerability to combat-related stressors.

## Combat-Specific Differences

Women's increased exposure to combat in OEF/OIF provides a unique opportunity to better understand gender differences in the mental health consequences of combat exposure. Though no published studies have examined differential associations for women and men in an OEF/OIF sample, one study that took a slightly different approach to this research question produced several interesting findings. In a sample of infantry and combat support service members women were significantly more likely than men to screen positive for general mental health problems when exposure to combat was low (17% compared to 9%), but there was no difference under moderate levels of combat exposure. While this study provides some support for the possibility of gender differences in the impact of combat exposure on postdeployment mental health, it also suggests that this effect may be small.

Prior research has revealed four categories of combat-related stress that may be especially important to consider in research in this area. These factors include: (a) combat exposure; (b) exposure to the aftermath of battle; (c) perceived threat; and (d) difficult living and working environment. Among these stressors, combat exposure has received the greatest attention in the literature. Studies based on OEF/OIF service members, as well as prior cohorts, indicate that combat exposure, including experiences such as being fired upon and witnessing death, has significant implications for postdeployment mental health. Exposure to the aftermath of battle, such as handling human remains or caring for injured personnel, has received less direct research attention though several studies based on OEF/OIF service members indicate that these experiences are associated with poor postdeployment mental health. Of note, research has revealed different correlates and consequences of combat exposure and aftermath of battle, underscoring the importance of examining these dimensions separately.

## The Role of Perception of Threat

Perceptions of threat in the war zone have also been implicated in the mental health of returning service members. In a study using data from the National Vietnam Veterans Readjustment Study, perceived threat of bodily harm or death played a key role in accounting for the postdeployment mental health of returning veterans. Findings suggest that this factor may also be relevant for the OEF/OIF cohort. For example, in a study of predictors of PTSD among health care providers deployed to Afghanistan and Iraq, [Tonya] Kolkow and colleagues found [in 2007] a strong association between concerns about danger and probable PTSD. Similarly,

[Katherine M.] Iversen et al. [in 2008] found that threat perceptions predicted PTSD in a sample of UK military personnel deployed to Iraq.

Another factor that may also be implicated in the postdeployment adjustment of returning OEF/OIF service members is ongoing exposure to the lower-level stress of living in a war zone. Aspects of the difficult living and working environment may include stressors such as long workdays and exposure to uncomfortable climates. Research based on both Vietnam veterans and Gulf War veterans has documented the impact of this lower-level stressor on postdeployment health, though no studies on this topic were identified in the OEF/OIF veteran literature.

The goal of the present study was to examine gender differences in different dimensions of combat-related stress and their associated relationship with postdeployment mental health in a national sample of female and male U.S. OEF/OIF veterans. This study builds on prior research in this area in a number of ways. First, this study focused on a sample in which there was ample dispersion in women's combat exposure to allow for gender comparisons across comparable levels of combat. Second, consistent with recent recommendations in the literature, this study took a more fine-grained approach to conceptualizing combat-related stress than has been typical in the literature. Third, both sampling weights and nonresponse bias weights were applied to produce results that would be optimally representative of the larger population. Prior research has primarily relied on convenience samples and has not taken into consideration the impact of non-response bias on study findings.

Stemming from the recognition that warfare exposure has broad-ranging impacts on mental health, gender differences in associations between different dimensions of combat-related stress and posttraumatic stress symptomatology (PTSS), depression, substance abuse, and mental health functional status were examined in addition to evaluating mean gender differences on combat-related stressors. These analyses controlled for additional stressors—namely, prior life stress exposure and deployment sexual harassment—to isolate unique relationships between combat-related stressors and different aspects of postdeployment mental health. Based on the literature on gender differences in combat exposure among OEF/OIF service members, we hypothesized that men would report significantly more exposure to combat-related stressors than women, but that effect sizes associated with these differences would be small. Based on research indicating that women may be somewhat more vulnerable to the effects of combat exposure, we hypothesized that combat-related stressors would demonstrate a significantly stronger negative impact on postdeployment mental health for women than men, but that this effect would also be small. . . .

## Small Differences Between Genders

Study findings revealed a number of important findings with respect to gender differences in exposure to combat-related stressors and associated relationships with postdeployment mental health among U.S. OEF/OIF service members. As expected, men reported more exposure to the three more objective combat-related stressors examined in this study. The fact that these differences were relatively small, however, suggests that women's exposure to these stressors in OEF/OIF may be only slightly lower than men's exposure, on average. This finding is consistent with anecdotal reports suggesting high levels of combat exposure for female service members, and indicates that policies barring women from ground combat roles may be less meaningful in modern warfare, where combat exposure is often indirect and difficult to predict due to the enemy's use of guerilla warfare tactics. This finding is of particular significance given the recent call for the Pentagon to reverse its long-standing policy barring women from ground combat, which can limit women's career advancement in the military. This finding also highlights the need for increased attention to women's experiences of combat-related stress in the assessment and treatment of returning OEF/OIF veterans in both VA and DoD health-care settings.

Despite lower levels of combat exposure, women reported similar levels of subjective perceived threat in the war zone as men. It is possible that women's increased vulnerability to other stressors in the war zone, including sexual harassment, may have increased their perceptions of threat to levels that were comparable to that reported by men. In addition, given that all service members are at risk of combat exposure in these wars, it is perhaps not surprising that women report comparable levels of concern regarding their safety and well-being in the war zone. It may also be that the threshold for experiencing threat is lower for women than men, as suggested by a number of psychophysiological studies.

Contrary to our hypothesis that associations between combat-related stressors and postdeployment mental health would be slightly stronger for women than men, only one of 16 interactions achieved a conventional level of statistical significance and this interaction suggested a stronger negative association for men rather than women. This finding is important because it appears to suggest fairly comparable levels of resilience to combat-related stressors for women and men, at least during the timeframe evaluated in this study....

## Combat Is an Equalizer

The conclusion that gender differences in the impact of combat-related stressors on mental health are minimal is consistent with comments offered ... in ... recent commentary on women in combat. These authors suggested that combat duty may be a great equalizer of risk due to its persistent level of threat. The lack of clinically significant gender differences may also, to some extent, reflect improved training of female service members in recent years. This interpretation is consistent with the finding that perceptions of preparedness for deployment did not differ for men and women in this sample. Regardless of the cause, these findings have substantial implications for military policy, as they call into question the commonly held belief that women may be more vulnerable to the negative effects of combat exposure than men.

Although not a primary focus of the study, it was interesting to note that different combat-related stressors were implicated in different dimensions of postdeployment mental health. Particularly noteworthy was the finding that combat exposure was not uniquely associated with any of the four mental health dimensions assessed in this study in regressions, though it was associated with mental health measures in bivariate correlations. This finding suggests that the relationship observed between objective combat circumstances and postdeployment mental health in studies that do not assess other combat-related stressors may be explained, at least in part, by combat's association with other aspects of the war-zone experience. Consistent with this perspective, perceived threat has been identified as a key mediator of the impact of combat exposure on PTSD in different cohorts. These findings underscore the importance of measuring a wide range of combat-related stressors in research on deployment stress and highlight the need for clinicians to attend to a broad range of combat-related stressors in both assessment and treatment. . . .

## Study Findings

In conclusion, study findings suggest that both exposure to combat-related stressors and their associated impact on postdeployment mental health in the year following return from deployment may be more similar than different for female and male U.S. service members. This finding is striking given that it contrasts with the widely accepted view that women are

## Post-Traumatic Stress Disorder (PTSD)

PTSD can occur after you have been through a traumatic event. Professionals do not know why it occurs in some and not others. But we do know PTSD is treatable.

Symptoms of PTSD:

*Re-experiencing*

Bad memories of a traumatic event can come back at any time. You may feel the same terror and horror you did when the event took place. Sometimes; there's a trigger: a sound, sight, or smell that causes you to relive the event.

*Avoidance and Numbing*

People with PTSD often go to great lengths to avoid things that might remind them of the traumatic event they endured. They also may shut themselves off emotionally in order to protect themselves from feeling pain and fear.

*Hypervigilance or Increased Arousal*

Those suffering from PTSD may operate on "high-alert" at all times, often have very short fuses, and startle easily.

*US Department of Veterans Affairs,*
*"Returning from the War Zone,"*
*September 2010. www.ptsd.va.gov.*

more vulnerable to the negative impact of trauma exposure than men. Future research is needed to promote a better understanding of the factors that may contribute to similar levels of resilience to combat trauma among female and male U.S. service members deployed in support of OEF/OIF, as well as the limits of this phenomenon.

"There are no time limits for being eligible for free, [Military Sexual
Trauma]-related care, which means
Veterans can seek treatment even many
years after discharge."

# Servicewomen Have Access to Benefits and Treatment for Military Sexual Trauma

*US Department of Veterans Affairs*

*The US Department of Veterans Affairs provides physical and mental health services, as well as support services for all US veterans. In the following viewpoint, the VA describes the experiences of two veterans who have found successful treatment for Military Sexual Trauma (MST) through accessing VA services. Services for victims of MST are wide-ranging, free of charge, and are regularly accessible, even to veterans who are not able to access other VA services. Further, there are no time limits for beginning treatment, so veterans who served decades earlier can still access treatment for MST. The VA encourages anyone suffering from MST to seek help as soon as possible, and contends that help is available to anyone living anywhere in the country who suffers from MST.*

"Don't Suffer in Silence: VA Offers Help for Military Sexual Trauma (MST)," My HealtheVet, US Department of Veterans Affairs, Sept. 17, 2012.

As you read, consider the following questions:

1. What does Jennifer Norris say was the beginning of her journey to healing, as cited by the VA?

2. Why does Rowdy Grigsby, as cited by the author, say that it is hard for soldiers to surrender to the idea that they need help?

3. How many programs nationwide does the VA have that offer specialized MST treatment?

It took two long years, but Air National Guard Veteran Jennifer Norris finally found the courage and support she needed to report she had been raped by her recruiter and sexually assaulted by three other superiors and fellow Servicemembers while on active duty.

"One of my superiors said my performance went from excellent to 'I don't give a darn anymore,'" said Norris. "He was concerned and wondered what was going on, so he asked me." Norris, who by that time had reached her "breaking point," came clean about what had happened. That was the beginning of her journey toward healing.

## Wide-Reaching Effects

Both women and men experience military sexual trauma (MST). MST is the term the Department of Veterans Affairs (VA) uses to refer to sexual assault or sexual harassment that occurred while the Veteran was in the military. MST can have a long-term impact on a survivor's mental and physical health, with common aftereffects including anger, depression, anxiety and substance abuse. The trauma may also affect relationships with family, friends and coworkers, as well as work attendance and performance.

"PTSD [post-traumatic stress disorder] is the most common diagnosis related to MST among both male and female Veterans, but survivors have a wide variety of responses," said

Dr. Ashley Niehaus, a member of the VA's national MST Support Team, funded by the VA's Office of Mental Health Services.

Norris, who developed a problem with alcohol, first turned to a private therapist for help. But when, by chance, she found a card with a VA MST counselor's name and contact information on it, she called. "I didn't know there were VA resources available to me," said Norris. "It was like a lifeline."

Though her private therapist helped her address her drinking problem, she was unfamiliar with the military, according to Norris. "The VA totally understood how the military works—that was huge. By stepping into the VA, I stepped into my own world. The VA educated me about PTSD and the triggers and told me what I was going through was a common response to MST. They validated me and helped me talk about it."

## Screening for MST Is Mandated

"It's important that VA be a place where Veterans feel comfortable discussing their experiences of MST with providers," said Dr. Margret Bell, acting Director for Education and Training with VA's national MST Support Team. To ensure this happens, VA provides its clinical staff with in-depth training about the impact of MST. It has also established policies that all Veterans seen for health care services must be asked if they experienced MST so they can be informed of the specialized services VA has available. In addition to seeing a VA MST counselor for outpatient treatment, Norris attended a six-week, inpatient VA PTSD program. She also started a blog, "Justice for MST Survivors," and joined a VA writers' group led by a VA facilitator. The group, which meets every two weeks, includes mostly Veterans coping with PTSD. "We're going to turn our stories into theater productions, which will premiere on Veteran's Day," said Norris.

Writing also helps Army Veteran Rowdy Grigsby, who composes "PTSD poetry." After a long road to recovery that included a stay in a VA transitional program for the homeless, Grigsby—who also suffered from MST and PTSD—said his life has changed "100 percent."

## Get Help as Soon as Possible

Both Grigsby and Norris described reaching a "breaking" or "tipping" point before seeking help. Seeking treatment earlier can prevent prolonged suffering and problems such as homelessness, unemployment and broken relationships. "You have to reach that point where you have to surrender to the idea that you need help," said Grigsby. "It's hard because we're soldiers, and we're taught not to give up."

## VA Services for MST Survivors

If you are a Veteran and have MST, here are some things you should know:

- All VA treatment for physical and mental health conditions related to MST is free

- Veterans do not need to be service connected (have a VA disability rating) to have reported the abuse at the time it occurred or to have other proof of MST in order to receive free care for MST-related conditions

- There are no time limits for being eligible for free, MST-related care, which means Veterans can seek treatment even many years after discharge

- Veterans may be eligible for free, MST-related care even if they are not eligible for other VA services

- Every VA health care facility has an MST coordinator who can answer any questions you might have about VA's MST-related services and help you access VA programs

- Every VA health care facility has providers knowledgeable about treatment for problems related to MST.
Many facilities have specialized outpatient mental
health services focusing on sexual trauma. VA Centers
also have specially trained sexual trauma counselors

- VA has almost two dozen programs nationwide that
offer specialized MST treatment in a residential or inpatient setting. These programs are for Veterans who
need more intense treatment and support. Because
some Veterans do not feel comfortable in mixed-gender
treatment settings, some facilities have separate programs for men and women. All residential and inpatient MST programs have separate sleeping areas for
men and women. . . .

"It's important for Veterans to know that there's hope—
recovery is possible—and that VA can help," said Niehaus.

> *"The VA only approves one in three claims for [post-traumatic stress disorder] stemming from military sexual trauma."*

# Servicewomen Are Routinely Denied Access to Benefits and Treatment for Military Sexual Trauma

*Molly O'Toole*

*Molly O'Toole is a news editor with the* Huffington Post. *In the following viewpoint, she reports on the introduction in the Senate of the Ruth Moore Act of 2013, a bill aimed at improving the claim approval process for victims of military sexual trauma (MST) and facilitating an easier process by which victims can access treatment through the VA. O'Toole cites sources indicating that the VA routinely rejects claims for PTSD treatment caused by MST and frequently gives women a lower disability rating (which determines their level of benefits) than it gives men. Help for MST survivors is needed to obtain treatment and benefits they have been denied, and to keep victims from being labeled as mentally ill and discharged without benefits, as so many MST survivors are, O'Toole concludes.*

As you read, consider the following questions:

1. How many reported sexual assaults were there in the military in 2011, according to O'Toole?

2. How many claims for PTSD stemming from MST does the VA approve, according to SWAN, as cited by the author?

3. What disability rating are women more likely to receive than men, according to O'Toole?

Ruth Moore's career in the military began like many others: at age 18, she joined the Navy, "eager to fight" for her country. But two and a half months later, her supervisor raped her multiple times, Moore says, and she began her fight against the Department of Defense and the Veterans Administration [VA] to get full disability benefits.

Now, nearly three decades later, an act bearing her name has been introduced to assist survivors of military sexual assault in securing their VA benefits from the Department of Veterans Affairs. Sen. Jon Tester (D-Mont.) and Rep. Chellie Pingree (D-Maine) put forth the Ruth Moore Act of 2013 Wednesday afternoon [February 13, 2013], a day after President Barack Obama pledged in the State of the Union to continue improving health care for veterans and expanding opportunities for women in combat.

## The Ruth Moore Act

"Survivors of military sexual assault and sexual harassment are betrayed twice: first by the military who all too often fails to support the victim, and by the VA, which has for years systematically rejected MST [military sexual trauma] disability claims based on this unequal and unfair regulation," Anu Bhagwati, executive director of Service Women's Action Network (SWAN) and a former Marine Corps captain, said in a statement to *The Huffington Post*. Bhagwati introduced the bill with Tester and Pingree.

In addition to improving the claims process, the Ruth Moore Act aims to relax standards of evidence for tying an applicant's mental health state to an assault. For example, the bill would allow a mental health professional's examination to serve as evidence of military sexual assault, since creating, obtaining or maintaining official records of it have proven difficult at both Defense and the VA. The draft legislation would shift the burden of proof, directing decisions to be made with "every reasonable doubt in favor of the veteran," the *Army Times* reports. The bill will also require the VA to report MST claim statistics annually to Congress.

## One in Three Servicewomen

According to the Defense Department, as many as one in three servicewomen report having been sexually assaulted. In fiscal year 2011, there were 3,192 reported sexual assaults with both female and male victims, but the Pentagon estimates that more than 86 percent of military sexual assault incidents are never reported. Defense projects that some 19,000 assaults occurred—more than 50 a day.

The Government Accountability Office concluded two weeks ago that while Defense has taken steps forward, immediate action is needed to correct the lack of medical and mental health care for victims of sexual assault. According to SWAN, the VA only approves one in three claims for PTSD [post-traumatic stress disorder] stemming from military sexual trauma, the VA's preferred term for the physical and mental fallout faced by survivors. Bhagwati testified before Congress last year [2012] that women are more likely to receive a lower disability rating—of 10 to 30 percent—whereas men are more

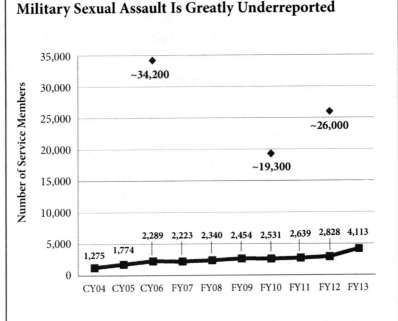

**Military Sexual Assault Is Greatly Underreported**

◆ Estimated Number of Service Members Experiencing Unwanted Sexual Contact Using DMDC WGRA Survey Past-Year Prevalence Rates

■ Service Member Victims in Reports of Sexual Assault to DoD Authorities for Incidents That Occurred in Military Service (Unrestricted and Restricted)

Note: Estimated service members experiencing unwanted sexual contact based on survey prevalence rates vs. number of service member victims in reports of sexual assault made during the fiscal year, for incidents occurring while in military service

TAKEN FROM: US Department of Defense, *Annual Report on Sexual Assault in the Military, Fiscal Year 2013*, April 2014.

likely to receive a 70 to 100 percent disability rating, which helps determine the benefits for which a veteran is eligible.

## The VA Argues Its Case

Victoria Dillon, deputy press secretary for the Department of Veterans Affairs, said in a statement that the VA is "committed" to helping veterans get the necessary health care.

"For Military Sexual Trauma disability claims, VA's regulations are liberal and designed to ensure that all available evidence supporting these claims is considered," Dillon said. "Because military service records may lack corroborating evidence that an event occurred, VA regulations make clear that evidence from other sources may be used to corroborate the Veteran's account of the incident.

"We are aware that draft legislation was discussed today regarding VA's disability claims process for Military Sexual Trauma. VA will review the legislation, and if requested by Congress, provide official views on the measure."

## Survivors of MST Are Mistreated

The Navy discharged Moore after [she] attempted suicide, diagnosing her with borderline personality disorder, according to the *Army Times*. Getting discharged with a mental illness diagnosis is common among victims of military sexual assault. Moore's initial applications for disability benefits were denied and subsequent applications granted varying levels of disability. She is now rated as a 100 percent disabled veteran, about 25 years later.

Survivors of military sexual assault have limited means of recourse. Just last week, in one of several cases that have been brought against the Department of Defense, the United States District Court for the District of Columbia Circuit ruled that the defendants—including outgoing Defense Secretary Leon Panetta—are entitled to qualified immunity, which protects government officials from liability in civil suits. The ruling deemed that the plaintiffs' assaults were "incident to military service," and stated that the Department of Defense did not have "a constitutional duty to protect [plaintiffs] from sexual assault and retaliation committed by other service members."

"We have a responsibility to meet the needs of all victims of service-related trauma," Tester, a member of the Senate Veterans' Affairs Committee, said in a statement to *HuffPost*.

"This legislation is simply a matter of fairness to make sure that survivors of military sexual assault get the support they deserve without having to jump through additional hoops."

Pingree noted in a statement that widespread sexual assault, rather than the claims process, is the primary issue.

"It's outrageous that men and women who sign up to defend our country end up being victims of sexual assault in the first place," Pingree said. "Then to deny them the help they need to recover is simply unacceptable . . . It's a classic case of adding insult to injury."

# Periodical and Internet Sources Bibliography

*The following articles have been selected to supplement the diverse views presented in this chapter.*

| Meena Hart Duerson | "Woman Says She Was Kicked Out of the Air Force for Being Pregnant, Told She Could Have Served If She'd Had an Abortion," *New York Daily News*, October 25, 2012. |
| --- | --- |
| Glenda Fauntleroy | "Women Veterans Report Poorer Health Despite Access to Health Services, Insurance," Center for Advancing Health, April 10, 2012. www.cfah.org. |
| James Kitfield | "The Enemy Within," *National Journal*, September 13, 2012. |
| LifeNews.com | "Democrats Pushing to Fund Abortions on US Military Bases," December 13, 2012. www.lifenews.com. |
| David S. Martin | "Rape Victims Say Military Labels Them 'Crazy,'" CNN, April 14, 2012. www.cnn.com. |
| Rick Nauert | "Past Physical, Sexual Attack Ups Risk of Military Suicide," PsychCentral, January 22, 2013. http://psychcentral.com. |
| Julia Savacool | "Military Women: Home Safe but Not Sound," *Women's Health*, April 3, 2012. |
| Leo Shane III | "VA Benefits Process Called 'Unrealistic' for Military Sex Assault Victims," *Stars and Stripes*, July 18, 2012. |
| Gregg Zoroya | "Army Task Force: Female Troops Need Better Health Care," *USA Today*, June 18, 2012. |

# For Further Discussion

## Chapter 1

1. Andrea Flynn claims that the Republican Party's policies interfere with women's health and personal freedom, while Meghan Clyne blames such interference on the Democratic party. Renee Parsons blames both political parties and claims that they are using opposing views on abortion and contraception to distract voters from their actual agendas to garner votes. After reading all three viewpoints, does it seem that Flynn and Clyne might engage in the kind of rhetoric that Parsons opposes? Explain.

2. *Scientific American* argues that Planned Parenthood's public funding is both justified and needed, because the organization provides vital preventive health services for women apart from abortion. Tony Perkins contends that Planned Parenthood's claim to provide nonabortion services is inaccurate and that the group does not deserve public funding. Dominic A. Carone argues that health service organizations like Planned Parenthood that receive public funding should expect controversy when they take sides in contentious political debates. Based on what you have read in these three viewpoints, do you think that it is appropriate for publicly funded health service organizations to take a stance for or against political issues? If so, do you think that taking a stance should preclude them from receiving public funding? Why or why not? If not, do you think that not taking a stance entitles them to receive public funding? Explain.

## Chapter 2

1. Michael McConnell says that according to the Religious Freedom Restoration Act, the government is required to use the least restrictive means of ensuring that all women

have access to affordable reproductive services and that requiring churches and religiously affiliated hospitals that regard such services as morally wrong to provide them to their employees violates this law. The National Women's Law Center maintains that refusing to provide women with birth control and emergency reproductive services because of religious objections to these services constitutes imposing religious beliefs on someone and is thus a violation of a woman's constitutional right to freedom from religion. What do you think? Does the Religious Freedom Restoration Act guarantee religious employers the right to refuse to provide employees with birth control or for hospitals to refuse to provide emergency reproductive services? Explain. Does this law conflict with the First Amendment clause guaranteeing religious freedom? Why or why not?

2. After reading the viewpoints by Denise M. Burke and Anna Franzonello, Jeff Fortenberry, Nitzan Weizmann, and Jodi Jacobson, how do you think government could best compromise to safeguard the rights both of those who support coverage of birth control under the Affordable Care Act and of those who oppose such coverage based on religious objections? Explain your answer using examples from the viewpoints in chapter 2.

# Chapter 3

1. Does the viewpoint by Genevra Pittman undermine the argument against the US Preventive Services Task Force's mammography guidelines in Elisa Rush Port's viewpoint? Why or why not? Explain.

2. Britt Wahlin supports the ability of women to purchase birth control pills without a prescription, while Morgan Greenwald argues against it. Which argument do you find more compelling? Why?

# Chapter 4

1. After reading the viewpoints by the US Government Accountability Office and the Women's Health Assessment Team, do you think that the Department of Defense is providing adequate health care for deployed servicewomen? Why or why not? If you think that the services are not adequate, what could the Department of Defense do to improve their services?

2. Bari Walsh presents commentary that suggests that military women are at greater risk of developing PTSD than are military men, while Dawne Vogt and associates indicate that there is no difference in the rate of combat-related PTSD between genders. Which author do you think offers the more persuasive argument? Why? Are there more similarities or more differences between their arguments? Based on the information provided in both viewpoints, do you think that women should be allowed to serve in combat? Explain your reasoning.

# Organizations to Contact

*The editors have compiled the following list of organizations concerned with the issues debated in this book. The descriptions are derived from materials provided by the organizations. All have publications or information available for interested readers. The list was compiled on the date of publication of the present volume; names, addresses, phone and fax numbers, and e-mail and Internet addresses may change. Be aware that many organizations take several weeks or longer to respond to inquiries, so allow as much time as possible.*

**American Association of University Women (AAUW)**
1111 Sixteenth St. NW, Washington, DC  20036
(202) 785-7700
e-mail: connect@aauw.org
website: www.aauw.org

AAUW has worked for more than 120 years to increase the access of women and girls to higher education and to ensure gender equity in institutes of higher learning. The group publishes its research on the way various issues affect women and girls, offers grants and fellowships, and maintains leadership programs.

**American Life League (ALL)**
PO Box 1350, Stafford, VA  22555
(540) 659-4171 • fax: (540) 659-2586
website: thepillkills.org

The American Life League's The Pill Kills campaign seeks to warn the public of the dangers of the birth control pill. ALL outlines the many side effects of the pill, citing specific cases of women suffering permanent physical damage and even death as a result of birth control pill use. ALL also warns that the pill is harmful to marriages, because it limits procreation, interrupts bonding between spouses, and lowers a woman's libido. The ALL website offers links to talking points, related news items, and opportunities to participate in protest activities opposing the use and sale of oral contraceptives.

## Association of Reproductive Health Professionals (ARHP)

1901 L St. NW, Ste. 300, Washington, DC   20036
(202) 446-3825
e-mail: arhp@arhp.org
website: www.arhp.org

The Association of Reproductive Health Professionals is a medical association comprising reproductive health professionals interested in networking and disseminating the most effective and up-to-date information on programs, policies, technology, and medical breakthroughs. The ARHP develops evidence-based programs for its members with the goal of providing the best care to their patients. The ARHP website offers interactive tools for patients searching for accurate information on contraception, sexually transmitted diseases, and other issues of reproductive health. The official journal of ARHP, *Contraception: An International Reproductive Health Journal*, features groundbreaking research and commentary on hot topics in reproductive health.

## Bixby Center for Global Reproductive Health

3333 California St., Ste. 225, Box 0744
San Francisco, CA   94143
(415) 502-4086 • fax: (415) 502-8479
website: bixbycenter.ucsf.edu

The Bixby Center for Global Reproductive Health was established in 1999 by the University of California–San Francisco to develop strategies to address domestic and international health problems. The center outlines its goals as formulating new reproductive health technologies in contraception and reproductive and maternal health, decreasing maternal mortality, training practitioners and researchers, conducting policy analyses and research in the field, and improving adolescent reproductive health. The Bixby Center website offers access to a range of reports on contraception and reproductive health, fact sheets, monographs and books, videos, and issue briefs.

## Center for Reproductive Rights (CRR)

120 Wall St., New York, NY  10005
(917) 637-3600 • fax: (917) 637-3666
e-mail: info@reprorights.org
website: reproductiverights.org

CRR is an organization of attorneys and activists focused on strengthening reproductive rights legislation throughout the United States as well as internationally. CRR has brought cases before state and district courts, the US Supreme Court, United Nations committees, and regional human rights groups, using international human rights law, the US Constitution, and the Universal Declaration of Human Rights as the basis for its arguments.

## Foundation for Gender-Specific Medicine

903 Park Ave., Ste. 2A, New York, NY  10075
(212) 737-5663 • fax: (212) 737-6306
e-mail: info@gendermed.org
website: www.gendermed.org

The Foundation for Gender-Specific Medicine supports the investigation of how gender affects normal human function and the experience of disease. Marianne J. Legato established the foundation to continue the work she began with the Partnership for Gender-Specific Medicine at Columbia University. The foundation supports original scientific research in gender-specific medicine, and works to create an evidence-based set of protocols to guide physicians in providing optimal gender-specific treatment and to educate both the public and the scientific/medical community in gender-specific medicine.

## NARAL Pro-Choice America

1156 Fifteenth St. NW, Ste. 700, Washington, DC  20005

(202) 973-3000 • fax: (202) 973-3096
website: www.prochoiceamerica.org

NARAL is a political advocacy group that lobbies for reproductive rights and legal abortion access through state and federal chapters throughout the United States.

### National Latina Institute for Reproductive Health (NLIRH)
50 Broad St., Ste. 1937, New York, NY 10004
(212) 422-2553 • fax: (212) 422-2556
e-mail: nlirh@latinainstitute.org
website: http://latinainstitute.org

The NLIRH works for reproductive justice for Latinas by addressing common social problems in the Hispanic American population, including poverty, unemployment, workplace discrimination, illegal alien status, and lack of educational opportunities. The organization achieves its goals by advocating for public policies that benefit Latinas and against those that target low-income women.

### National Organization for Women (NOW)
1100 H St. NW, 3rd fl., Washington, DC 20005
(202) 628-8669 • fax: (202) 785-8576
website: www.now.org

NOW was founded in 1966 and is the largest and perhaps best-known women's advocacy groups in the United States. NOW activism includes electoral lobbying and candidate endorsement in addition to its work forming policy and bringing legal action on behalf of women's issues, including women's health. NOW members also engage in acts of nonviolent protest such as marches and rallies.

### National Partnership for Women and Families
1875 Connecticut Ave. NW, Ste. 650, Washington, DC 20009
(202) 986-2600 • fax: (202) 986-2539
e-mail: info@nationalpartnership.org
website: www.nationalpartnership.org

The National Partnership for Women and Families was founded in 1971 as the Women's Legal Defense Fund, with the goal of battling sex-based discrimination of all forms in court. In 1998 the group changed its name to reflect its work on behalf of working families, including its long-running push for passage of the Family and Medical Leave Act, which was written by a staff attorney for the group in 1985 and signed into law by President Bill Clinton in 1993.

### National Women's Law Center (NWLC)
11 Dupont Circle NW, #800, Washington, DC   20036
(202) 588-5180 • fax: (202) 588-5185
e-mail: info@nwlc.org
website: www.nwlc.org

The NWLC was founded in 1972 as part of the Center for Law and Social Policy to address women's issues. In 1981 it became an independent organization. Among the issues the NWLC supports are equal pay and employment, Title IX and education funding, child care and early childhood learning, reproductive rights and access to health care, and women's poverty.

### Office on Women's Health (OWH)
US Department of Health and Human Services
Washington, DC   20201
(871) 696-6775
website: www.womenshealth.gov

The Office on Women's Health of the US Department of Health and Human Services was established in 1991 to improve the health of American women by advancing and coordinating a comprehensive women's health agenda. It addresses health care prevention and service delivery, research, education, and career advancement for women in the health professions and in scientific careers. The OWH also works with numerous government agencies, nonprofit organizations, consumer groups, and associations of health care professionals to ensure that all American women have access to reproductive care and other preventive health care services.

## Planned Parenthood Federation of America (PPFA)
434 W. Thirty-Third St., New York, NY   10001
(212) 541-7800 • fax: (212) 245-1845
website: www.plannedparenthood.org

Planned Parenthood was formed as the American Birth Control League in 1921 to promote the use and legalization of birth control in the United States. Currently, PPFA falls under the larger umbrella organization of the International Planned Parenthood Federation, operating eight hundred clinics across the United States that provide a wide variety of health services to women free of charge.

## Service Women's Action Network (SWAN)
220 E. Twenty-Third St., Ste. 509, New York, NY   10010
(646) 559-5200
e-mail: info@servicewomen.org
website: www.servicewomen.org

SWAN endeavors to transform military culture by advocating for equal opportunity for women in the military by fighting discrimination, sexual harassment, and sexual assault. SWAN advocates for reform for active military and veterans' health services, including preventive and emergency reproductive care, and mental health services.

## Women Veterans Health Program
US Department of Veterans Affairs, Washington, DC   20420
(855) 829-6636 (Women Veterans Hotline)
website: www.womenshealth.va.gov

The Women Veterans Health Program works to address the health care needs of women veterans and to ensure that timely, equitable, high-quality, comprehensive health care services are provided in a sensitive and safe environment at VA health facilities nationwide. The Women Veterans Health Program focuses on providing all eligible women veterans with comprehensive primary care; quality primary care providers; privacy, safety, dignity, and sensitivity to women-specific health-care needs; accessible and timely health care; up-to-date medical technology and equipment; and preventive and clinical care at a level of quality equal to that provided to male veterans.

# Bibliography of Books

Carolyn B. Allard and Melissa Platt, eds.
*Military Sexual Trauma: Current Knowledge and Future Directions.* London: Routledge, 2011.

Erika Bachiochi, ed.
*The Cost of "Choice": Women Evaluate the Impact of Abortion.* New York: Encounter Books, 2004.

Karen L. Baird
*Beyond Reproduction: Women's Health, Activism, and Public Policy.* Madison, NJ: Fairleigh Dickinson University Press, 2009.

Susan E. Bell
*DES Daughters: Embodied Knowledge and the Transformation of Women's Health Politics.* Philadelphia: Temple University Press, 2009.

Tanya Biank
*Undaunted: The Real Story of America's Servicewomen in Today's Military.* New York: New American Library, 2013.

Linda Bickerstaff
*Violence Against Women: Public Health and Human Rights.* New York: Rosen, 2010.

Carole H. Browner and Carolyn F. Sargent, eds.
*Reproduction, Globalization, and the State: New Theoretical and Ethnographic Perspectives.* Durham, NC: Duke University Press, 2011.

Allan Carlson
*Godly Seed: American Evangelicals Confront Birth Control, 1873–1973.* New Brunswick, NJ: Transaction, 2011.

Sherry F. Colb — *When Sex Counts: Making Babies and Making Law*. Lanham, MD: Rowman & Littlefield, 2007.

Nancy Ehrenreich — *The Reproductive Rights Reader*. New York: New York University Press, 2008.

Laura Eldridge — *In Our Control: The Complete Guide to Contraceptive Choices for Women*. New York: Seven Stories, 2010.

John M. Ensor — *Answering the Call: Saving Innocent Lives, One Woman at a Time*. Peabody, MA: Hendrickson, 2012.

Steven Epstein — *Inclusion: The Politics of Difference in Medical Research*. Chicago: University of Chicago Press, 2007.

Jeanne Flavin — *Our Bodies, Our Crimes: The Policing of Women's Reproduction in America*. New York: New York University Press, 2009.

Angel M. Foster and Lisa L. Wynn, eds. — *Emergency Contraception: The Story of a Global Reproductive Health Technology*. New York: Palgrave Macmillan, 2012.

Lori Freedman — *Willing and Unable: Doctors' Constraints in Abortion Care*. Nashville: Vanderbilt University Press, 2010.

Melissa Haussman
*Reproductive Rights and the FDA: The Battles over Birth Control, RU-486, and Morning-After Pills and the Gardasil Vaccine.* Westport, CT: Praeger, 2012.

Melissa Haussman
*Reproductive Rights and the State: Getting the Birth Control, RU-486, Morning-After Pills, and the Gardasil Vaccine to the US Market.* Santa Barbara, CA: Praeger, 2013.

Patrick Lee
*Abortion and Unborn Human Life.* Washington, DC: Catholic University of America Press, 2010.

Barbara L. Ley
*From Pink to Green: Disease Prevention and the Environmental Breast Cancer Movement.* New Brunswick, NJ: Rutgers University Press, 2009.

Daniel C. Maguire
*Sacred Choices: The Right to Contraception and Abortion in Ten World Religions.* Minneapolis: Augsburg Fortress, 2001.

Robin Marty and Jessica Mason Pieklo
*Crow After Roe: How "Separate but Equal" Has Become the New Standard in Women's Health and How We Can Change That.* Brooklyn, NY: Ig, 2013.

Ellen S. More, Elizabeth Fee, and Manon Parry, eds.
*Women Physicians and the Cultures of Medicine.* Baltimore: Johns Hopkins University Press, 2009.

Sue V. Rosser, ed.    *Diversity and Women's Health.*
Baltimore: Johns Hopkins University
Press, 2009.

Kate Seear    *The Makings of a Modern Epidemic:
Endometriosis, Gender, and Politics.*
Burlington, VT: Ashgate, 2014.

Rickie Solinger    *Reproductive Politics: What Everyone
Needs to Know.* New York: Oxford
University Press, 2012.

R.C. Sproul    *Abortion: A Rational Look at an
Emotional Issue.* Orlando, FL:
Reformation Trust, 2010.

Sarah
Weddington    *A Question of Choice:* Roe v. Wade
*Fortieth anniversary ed.* New York:
Feminist, 2013.

James E. Wise Jr.    *Women at War: Iraq, Afghanistan,
and Scott Baron    and Other Conflicts.* US Naval
Institute Press, 2006.

# Index

Women's Health

Ethical and Religious Directives
for Catholic Health Care Services, 71–72

**F**

Family planning services, 26–27,
48–49, 53, 104
Feminine urinary diversion de-
vices (FUDD), 159
First Amendment, 43, 71, 73–75,
89
Fluke, Sandra, 25, 30
Flynn, Andrea, 21–27
Fogel, Susan Berke, 79
Force Health Protection Assess-
ment, 157
Fortenberry, Jeff, 94–100
Fourteenth Amendment, 41
Fox News, 52
Frankel, Lois, 19
Franzonello, Anna, 81–93
Free Exercise Clause, 73–74
Fudge, Marcia, 19

**G**

Gallup poll, 34–35
Gender-specific hygiene counsel-
ing, 159
Genitourinary symptoms, 160
George, Francis Cardinal, 34
Gingrich, Newt, 42
Glezerman, Marek, 117
Gore, Al, 41
Government Accountability Office,
194
Goyal, Vinita, 142
Greenwald, Morgan, 130–134
Grigsby, Rowdy, 190

*Griswold v. Connecticut* (1965), 35
Growth and Opportunity Project,
22
Guerilla warfare, 183
Guide to Clinical Preventive Ser-
vices, 98
Gulf War, 156, 182
Guttmacher Institute, 76–80

**H**

*Haaretz* (newspaper), 116
Hansen, Leah, 133–134
*Harris v. McRae* (1980), 88
Head Start program, 25
Health Care Conscience Rights
Act (2013), 92
Health care refusals, 79
Health Resources and Services
Administration (HRSA), 86
Health Service Support (HSS),
157, 164
Health.com, 133
Healthcare Freedom of Conscience
Act, 85, 87
Holocaust survivors, 169
Hormonal disorders, 105
*Hosanna-Tabor v. EEOC* (2012),
65
House Oversight and Government
Reform Committee, 102, 108
Howard, David, 128–129
*Huffington Post* (website), 194, 196
Hutcherson, Hilda, 133

**I**

In vitro fertilization, 71
Independent Duty Hospital
Corpsman, 149

216

Respect for Rights of Conscience Act (2011), 96–97
Reuters Health, 126, 129
Revolutionary War, 156
RH Reality Check (website), 23
Richards, Ann, 16, 56
Richards, Cecile, 16, 30, 51–52, 53, 56
Rifampin drug, 132
*Roe v. Wade* (1973), 19, 35, 41, 87
Roman Catholics, 64, 82
Romney, Mitt, 25, 36–38, 41–42, 47
Roosevelt, Theodore, 40
RU-486 pill, 85
Russian Women's Battalions of Death, 179
Ruth Moore Act (2013), 193–194
Ryan, Paul, 25, 29, 38

# S

SAFE providers, 164
Sanger, Margaret, 46
Santorum, Rick, 25, 42
Scalia, Antonin, 74
*Scientific American* (magazine), 45–49
Self-care benefits, 161–162
Self-determination, 32–34
Senate Veterans' Affairs Committee, 196
Service Women's Action Network (SWAN), 194
Sex-selective abortion, 36
Sexual assault
    barriers to reporting, 163–164
    prevention measures, 164–165
    as serious problem, 162–163
    victim care, 152–154

*See also* Military sexual trauma, Rape
Sexual Assault Response Coordinators and Victim Advocates, 152, 154
Sexual harassment, 171, 183–184, 188, 193
Sexual Harassment/Assault Response and Prevention Afghanistan Theater of Operations (SHARP ATO), 163–164, 165
Sexually transmitted infections, 142
Shanawani, Hasan, 62
Single-parent families, 29, 35
Sleep medication, 152
Snowe, Olympia, 41
Street, Amy, 171, 174
Sun Tzu, 29
Supplemental Nutrition Assistance Program (SNAP), 33
Susan G. Komen for the Cure, 56–57, 121

# T

Targeted Regulation of Abortion Providers (TRAP) laws, 19
Tea Party Republicans, 25
Temporary Assistance for Needy Families (TANF), 33
Tester, Jon, 193, 194, 196
Texas Senate Education Committee, 24
Third Country Nationals, 164
Title X Abortion Provider Prohibition Act, 53
Townhall.com, 15